Finding Your Inner Gold

A Gold Medal Paralympian's Secrets to Success

Carol Cooke AM

First published by Busybird Publishing 2017
Copyright © 2017 Carol Cooke

ISBN 978-1-925585-44-5

Carol Cooke has asserted her right under the Copyright, Designs and Patents Act 1988 to be identified as the author of this work. The information in this book is based on the author's experiences and opinions. The publisher specifically disclaims responsibility for any adverse consequences, which may result from use of the information contained herein. Permission to use information has been sought by the author. Any breaches will be rectified in further editions of the book.

All rights reserved. No part of this publication may be reproduced, stored in or introduced into a retrieval system, or transmitted in any form, or by any means (electronic, mechanical, photocopying, recording or otherwise) without the prior written permission of the author. Any person who does any unauthorised act in relation to this publication may be liable to criminal prosecution and civil claims for damages. Enquiries should be made through the publisher.

Carol would like to acknowledge and thank Gregoria Todaro, whose illustrations appear in chapters 1–10, and Michael Bretherton, whose illustrations appear in chapters 11–13.

Cover image: Jeff Crow
Cover design: Kev Howlett, Busybird Publishing
Layout and typesetting: Busybird Publishing

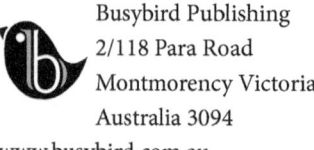

Busybird Publishing
2/118 Para Road
Montmorency Victoria
Australia 3094
www.busybird.com.au

DISCLAIMER: Every effort has been made to correctly attribute all quotes within. Any misattributions are unintentional.

Testimonials

'Carol is a motivational and inspirational speaker who appeals to many different audiences. Her exceptional ability to connect with her audience, and her thorough planning and preparation, ensures that each speaking engagement or professional activity is of the highest quality.'
Emma Sherry
– Senior Lecturer, La Trobe University

'I have heard Carol present to various audiences. She presents her story and relates it to the audience well. Carol is an inspirational speaker and is seen as a great leader. She uses stories from her various roles in life to show why people should try, even if they don't feel they will be able to achieve.'
Deidre McEwen
– Consulting Services Manager, IBM

'Carol is one of the most inspiring and motivating people I have met. She is an excellent public speaker who manages to grab the attentions of all ages. Her dedication and endless work for MS sufferers is an inspiration to all.'
Jane Wightman
– Administration Manager, Bovis Lend Lease

'Carol is an inspiration to everyone she meets due to her kind, caring and 'can do' approach to life. She has overcome significant adversity with her battles with Multiple Sclerosis to become a role model and now a Paralympic gold medallist in cycling. Carol is an exceptional presenter who engages the audience with touching stories about her life's journey, making you laugh and cry. I have no hesitation recommending Carol to any organisation that is seeking an inspirational motivational speaker. I will definitely be using Carol's services to inspire others.'

– **Bill Younger**
Foundation Director, St Vincent's Hospital Foundation

'Carol Cooke is an inspirational athlete and person. I have seen her in the training environment, at fundraising activities and when speaking to large groups. Carol inspires all those who have the good fortune to meet her. Her presentations to groups are professional and spellbinding. Her ability to motivate people is second to none and her success in the sporting arena is inspirational.'

– **Lisa Hasker**
Sport Manager, La Trobe University

'I had the pleasure of touring (insurance roadshow) with Carol for two weeks back in 2010. Travelling with Carol, I was able to see in person how she resonates with our clients, our audience. Carol is a great motivational speaker who knows the importance of a well-prepared speech. Working with Carol was a great pleasure for both my company and our clients.'

– **Goran Lazic**
Head of Medical Support Services, AMP

'Carol is a brilliant speaker who can capture the audience's attention and take them on an entertaining, meaningful and inspirational journey. Her messages are powerful, applicable to all of us and can be shared in any setting. I highly recommend her for your next event.'

   – George Halkias
   Sport for Development Professional, Educator, Speaker and Personal Development Facilitator

'Carol was an absolute privilege to have at our school as a guest speaker. Her presentation was warm and engaging, and her personal story was nothing short of inspirational. She left us with an invaluable message of resilience, which inspired our students to reflect on their approach to life by 'achieving their dream, believing in themselves and never giving up'. The children shared their thoughts and emotions by writing letters to Carol straight from the heart.'

   – Sandra McDonald
   Health and Physical Education Teacher, Taylors Lakes Primary School

'Carol Cooke is an inspirational figure to the many people she comes into contact with, whether they be people affected by Multiple Sclerosis, members of the sporting community or the general public.

'Her ability to cope with the effects of Multiple Sclerosis provides a living example of how a seemingly debilitating disease can be challenged, enabling a person to live a fulfilling life as part of a community.

'Carol's sporting achievements, as a swimmer, rower and Para-cyclist, provide ongoing inspiration not only to the

Paralympic movement but also to able-bodied athletes and the community. Carol is able to call upon her other life experiences as a police woman in Canada and her life with Multiple Sclerosis to become an inspirational speaker and motivator.

'Carol's deep understanding of life enables her to provide inspiration to groups ranging from senior management to school children.'
– **Greg Hutchings**
Development and Events Manager,
Multiple Sclerosis Ltd.

This book is dedicated to the numerous people who, throughout my life, have added value – be it good or bad – and who have taught me the many lessons that have enabled me to overcome challenges thrown at me.

To my family, who have helped shape me into the person I am.

To my husband, Russ, for being my rock and for holding down the fort when I go gallivanting 'round the world.

To my dear friend, Tina, who challenged me to write about my journey and to believe that I had something of value to share with the world.

And to my MS, which has made me the person I am today. Without a diagnosis of Multiple Sclerosis I don't believe that I would have had the privilege to experience the challenges and triumphs that I have had.

Contents

Introduction	i
Chapter 1: Inner Gold	1
Chapter 2: Unexpected Journey	13
Chapter 3: Change Happens	29
Chapter 4: Finding Courage	43
Chapter 5: Jumping Hurdles	57
Chapter 6: Ultimate Growth	69
Chapter 7: Winning Mindset	81
Chapter 8: Guaranteed Results	95
Chapter 9: Beyond Limits	107
Chapter 10: Discovering Gold	119
Chapter 11: Living Now	131
Chapter 12: Powerful Belief	141
Chapter 13: Celebrate Success	153
Afterword	165
About Carol	167
Email for Enquiries and Availability	169
Carol Cooke AM	170
Contact Details	172

Introduction

Do you know what your inner gold looks like? Have you looked deep within your heart to know the path you are on is the right one? Do you have goals in place to help find and reach that inner gold?

If you ever had to deal with change in your life, within your personal or you business life, you know that sometimes change can suck! How did you deal with it? Most of us don't deal with change very well. We tend to become complacent and like things as they are, as the old adage goes 'Why change it if it ain't broke!' Unfortunately life can sometimes have a way of changing things for you and it is that which I hope this book will help you through.

My life changed drastically a number of times with a few major changes and challenges, those being a move to the other side of the world and then again with what I thought at the time was a devastating diagnosis of a chronic illness. Compound the chronic illness with a cancer scare with major life changing surgery and you start to look at life a bit differently. So how did I deal with these changes and how did I find my inner gold are two of the questions I get asked the most when I am speaking to people.

If you are someone who struggles with setting goals and coping with change, it doesn't have to be a major event like mine but even the smaller things such as a new job or boss at work, then this book will give you some insight into how I challenge myself and deal with the changes in my life. It will also give you some strategies on how to cope with change and your mindset.

If you are struggling with finding that inner gold or lack the courage to try something new, wondering how I channel a winning mindset, interested in overcoming hurdles or how to celebrate your success then just go to that chapter on that topic. There is no right or wrong way to read this book.

I wrote this book because I have been able to find my inner gold and always seemed to be able to overcome challenges. It hasn't been easy but I have worked out ways to accept that change happens, get through the difficulties, find the courage to change, learn how to grow through the changes and have powerful belief in myself. At times I couldn't understand why everyone wasn't the same, why people were so scared of going after what they wanted and dealing with change.

I hope that when you read my thoughts and strategies told through stories in my life that you will understand that you don't have to be scared of your dreams, goals and change. That even though we may be fearful of attempting things or dealing with change we can eventually have amazing and wonderful outcomes.

Take the plunge, challenge yourself and you may actually find a new you, one who is brave and fearless, ready to take on anything the world has to throw at you.

Chapter 1:
Inner Gold

As I was called to the start line, the nervous energy was flowing through every fibre of my body. I don't think I had ever been so nervous at the start of a race. But this wasn't just any race … it was the 2016 Rio Paralympic women's T2 Road Race and I was about to race completely differently than I ever had before.

I had been beaten in 2015 at the Para Cycling World Championships for the first time since 2012 so it was important to learn how to race differently, learn tactics and learn how to take corners better than I ever had. Even though I had won the silver medal that year it was still a failure to me, but without failure we will never have success. I needed to find my inner gold through thinking outside the box and doing things differently.

So as I waited at the start in Rio for the gun to go off, my competitors were expecting me to do what I normally do and that was take off at the sound of the gun. But when the gun went off I stayed completely still and that forced the others to go at which time I slotted in at the back. The idea was to stay at the back watching what the others were doing and then towards the end of the race take off and try to drop all of my competitors. But I should know that things sometimes don't go to plan.

My German competitor had taken off and no one was going after her and so after a couple of kilometres when no one had gone, I broke from my protocol and sprinted away from the group to catch her. Most of the other girls came with me and we regrouped right behind her but that meant I wasn't at the back anymore. Still it occurred to me that I wasn't leading the group but my main competitor was now behind me.

It's important to remember that when things go wrong we have to think about how to right them. In the month before Rio I was training in Italy and had been practising different scenarios in regards to this race and what I would do. So at that point I again broke from what I had thought would be me sitting at the back most of the race and I took off as my German competitor was weaving across the road. I knew that some of the girls would come with me but I needed to see how many would come with me. After my quick sprint for about 30 seconds, I looked back and saw that there were now 5 of us. The problem was that I was now definitely on the front, but the scenarios we had practised kicked in. In order to get off the front of the bunch I weaved to the left and then quickly braked. The woman behind me hit my safety bar and the rest of them braked and weaved right which made them shoot past me. I was then able to slot back in to 4th wheel, so I was now back on track with my plan.

Usually when I am racing a road race I speak with the other riders but this time I kept silent and pretended I was deaf. I really wanted to do the opposite of everything I had ever done! I think this really un-nerved the others because as some of them tried to say something to me I just ignored them.

We had to do 2 laps of a 15km course which was very flat.

Chapter 1: Inner Gold

There were a couple of technical areas, one being a veer off the main road to the right and then a very sharp left hand turn, almost 180 degrees then right back onto the main road. After sitting on the back the first lap and seeing how difficult this turn was for most I decided that I had to be on the front at this point on the second lap. That would mean about 4km from the finish I had to really go for it.

As we crossed the start/finish line for the second lap, one of my main competitors, Jill, literally sat up, waved her arm, gesturing, and then yelled at me to take a turn at the front. I figured I had already done that the first lap by sprinting to catch the German and then sprinting to drop a couple of riders, so I sat on my trike keeping my mouth shut. Anyone that knows me would know that it was a very hard thing for me to do! Besides there are no rules in cycle racing saying that you had to take a turn on the front and she had done exactly that in 2015 when she just hung on to the back of me, racing past me on the last kilometre to beat me at World's.

With about 6.5 km's to the finish I saw Jill grab her water bottle and in that instant I thought, *Should I go and catch her off guard?* but that inner voice said, *No, it's too early.* She then started pulling at her jersey and then when I saw her move her chain up a gear it was very clear to me that she was getting ready to try and sprint away.

So with 5.5km to go, just a bit sooner than I wanted to go, I waited for the girls to weave to the right and I sprinted to the very far left side of the road. It was the plan to sprint for at least 40 seconds without looking back, go as hard as I could. I actually thought my head and lungs were going to explode! I have never gone so hard and the proof was in the data when I had finished. I had gone 150 watts of power better than I had ever gone ... no idea where that came from!

After about 45 seconds I looked back to see if anyone had come with me. Jill had tried to but I could see that if I kept it up I was going to break that invisible bungie cord that was between us. There was then a right-hand turn up around a 'dog leg' section and I kept the pressure up, not looking back once. As I came back down this section, I could see that she was about 600 metres behind and none of the other girls were with her. So, with only about 600 metres to go, I kept it up.

Our head coach Peter Day was screaming at me to slow down around the last left hand u-turn to the finish as I was far enough ahead. But to be honest slowing down was never in the plan! I did take the corner safely and was able to sprint down the home stretch on my own. As I crossed the line it was the most satisfying and emotional feeling I have ever had. People ask me what it feels like to win a Paralympic race and to be honest it is hard to describe. If you take all emotions possible and wrap them into one then you can understand. It had been an emotional year, with lots of highs and lows. The passing of my dad that March, winning in Europe, then my car being hit and written off by a texting driver and then making the team for Rio. All of those experiences plus the fact that I was trying something completely foreign to me by racing differently gave me that satisfying feeling and a huge overwhelming feeling of relief. I had found the gold within myself by not being fearful of trying something new. It had worked ... but even if it hadn't at least I would have known that I had tried my best.

I finished those Rio Paralympics with 2 gold medals. One

Chapter 1: Inner Gold

for the Time Trial and one the Road Race I just described and it was amazing to think that the dream I had as a 9 year old to represent my country at the highest level of sport had now not happened just once (2012) but twice! And to have 3 gold medals in my possession after 55 years of life, was to me, nothing short of a miracle.

Upon my return home, there was a lot of celebration, not only with family and friends but also the public, and I was also doing a lot of interviews and talks. It seemed like it was non stop, but it is important to celebrate our successes. I'm also not the type of athlete who hides their medals away in a safe deposit box, I like to share them, so I take them with me and share them around.

On the 26th of October, 2017 I had an interview and filming session with Monash University scheduled for around 11am. But I was trying to get back into some sort of training so was riding at 6 am with ladies from my cycling club. I decided to park at the Victorian Institute of Sport (VIS) in Albert Park, Melbourne. I knew that there would most likely be a staff member at the VIS by 6 am, so I had placed my Rio gold medals in the bottom of my bag with my wallet, my clothing for the day including my Australian team cycling kit, gym clothing and jeans, along with toiletries and one of the 'Tom's', the Rio Paralympic mascot presented to us with our medals. I had placed the bag in the footwell of the car. I didn't have anywhere else to put the bag as I had borrowed a car from MS and it was a very large station wagon with no boot. I did put the bag there before I got to the parking lot. I got myself ready to ride to meet the ladies and I made one big mistake ... I then placed my VIS jacket over the top of the bag.

Unfortunately a local criminal watched me do this and then after locking up the car I left the parking lot on my trike, that was at 5:42am. By 6am the first staff member arrived to find my car passenger window smashed. At 7:55 am I received a text message from my bank asking me if I had used a card to attempt to purchase $1000 worth of items online. I text back 'No' and they subsequently froze my accounts. At that time I figured that someone had stolen my wallet or the bank sent the message to the wrong person! In fact as I rolled up to my car about 15 minutes later I saw that the window had been broken.

The guy hadn't even opened the car door, just smashed the window and reached in to grab whatever it was that I had put my jacket over. He pulled the bag and my jacket through the window. I went through all the things that you do when someone has stolen your property. I called the bank to cancel other cards and called the police. As I was at the VIS, the marketing people called the press. We figured that if we could alert the media as soon as possible, then we might get lucky.

As I was waiting for the the police to arrive, the ABC and Chanel Seven crews arrived. The Seven News cameraman asked me why I wasn't upset. He said he would be stomping around swearing and yelling. It's a good thing he couldn't see what I was like inside because I was angry at myself, the criminal and the world, but I said to him, 'What would that accomplish?' It certainly wouldn't turn the clock back to stop the theft from happening. It wouldn't change the situation. I truly believe that sometimes crap just happens and how we deal with that crap defines who we are.

Chapter 1: Inner Gold

I had that many people asking me over and over again during the next few weeks 'Did you get your medals back?' And on the 12th of November, while at a training camp with the women from my cycling club, I finally just stood and said, 'Look, let's not talk about it anymore, the medals are gone, let's get over it. Not having the medals does not take away from what I have accomplished. They are just medals!'

I really do believe that when we can let the 'crap' in our life go things will then come back to us, because that night I received a voice message from a detective in Faulkner, Melbourne stating that I could stop looking for my medals because he was sitting staring at them. It had been 3 weeks but they had been found, after I decided to let go.

I had realised that my true 'Inner Gold' was still there, I'd had a dream, I'd worked to fulfil it and after years of attempting had finally succeeded. I didn't need an inanimate object to realise that I had found that inner gold.

Finding our Inner Gold is similar in many ways to actually making gold.

Just like miners who look for gold, they must dig deep, in fact half a kilometre underground. They know what they are looking for. We all need to know what our own gold looks like, we have to dig deep within our own hearts to find out what it is that we truly desire or dream of.

Making gold isn't easy, they have to drill holes in a pattern set out by engineers. Just like reaching our own inner gold we have to have a specific set of goals in order to train and fuel our bodies and minds to have the stamina to succeed.

Engineers know exactly where the veins are thanks to geologists who study ore samples, so in order to find a way to find our way to accomplishing our dreams we need to find the right coach or mentor who knows what it means to succeed and can help us along the right path.

Gold isn't pure and mined ore has to be processed to isolate the gold, just like no one is perfect at what they do. You have to enter into a process to isolate weaknesses that need to be worked on.

After blasting and crushing the rocks a number of times it is then ground to pulp, with chemicals and water added through more processes it is put under extreme heat where the gold separates. Gold does not become gold after just one process. As for finding our own inner gold you have to remember that failing at one step does not make you a failure, it can take years of getting back up, re-evaluating your progress and making changes as necessary.

In the end Gold takes about four minutes to solidify and another hour to cool completely – at this stage the gold is 80% pure and the mint will refine it to 99%. For us finding our inner gold, we can work until we are 80% there and then it is all about the little one percenters. Those little things are what will finally help us reach that final goal. It's important that we think outside the box when it comes to getting to these last steps and when you put effort and heart into realising that one dream, that hard work will result in skills that help you achieve others.

Chapter 1: Inner Gold

To find your inner gold take the following steps:

- Know what your gold looks like

- Set specific goals

- Find the right coach or mentor

- Understand your weaknesses and how to work on them

- If you fail, get back up and make changes as necessary

- Work on those 1% issues and think outside the box

- Never focus on the negative

Never let the odds of success be your focus because anything is possible. A metric tonne of ore usually only yields 6.5 grams of gold. So I am a good example of where anything is possible because to compete at the Paralympics is a 1 in 1.75 million chance. It all comes down to effort versus outcome!

Chapter 2:
Unexpected Journey

Have you ever had a dream? Well, after having a dream for forty-one years, over two countries, through three sports and one devastating diagnosis, I finally heard the words 'Congratulations on an amazing race. You just won the Paralympic gold!' With a stunned look, I turned to Genni, the Australian Paralympic Committee media rep, who said, 'I've been trying to tell you that for the last ten minutes.' With those words, I burst into tears. It was the 5th of September 2012 and I felt an almost instantaneous sense of relief. I had never let go of my dream of representing my country and I had finally done that, with the icing on the cake being that gold medal.

I was born Carol Lynn Banks on the 6th of August 1961, at the Grace Hospital in Toronto, Canada. I was the first child of Phyllis and Donald Banks, who had married the year before. My sister Cindy was born two years later and our family was complete. I had a wonderful childhood growing up in a new neighbourhood called Guildwood Village, in the suburbs of Toronto. Cindy and I were the only two girls on the street who played daily with all the local boys. During summer, it wasn't unusual for us to play rough-house tag with a few pokes and jabs. We also played baseball and street hockey with the guys. During winter we would build snow forts, have snowball fights and skate on the rink Dad had made in the backyard.

Right from the beginning I was taught to stand up for myself and question things. I was pigheaded and stubborn, which I am sure drove my parents nuts, but I believe that these qualities have helped me cope throughout my life and through all the different directions life has taken me.

I was involved in sport right from an early age and, while watching the Olympics at a very young age, decided that I wanted to be a gymnast. I had been taking part in gymnastics since age 4 and, around 9 years old, I decided I wanted to try out for an elite club. This was my first foray into 'elite' sport. Unfortunately, I didn't make the cut and, at this young age, was told I was too fat and had the wrong body type. Talk about devastating! No one had ever told me I was fat before. But I really believe this put me on a very long road to learning to love my body type. It has taken me about forty years to do so. Although I struggled with my body image and self-esteem, I didn't let it stop me from getting into other sports.

Growing up, my mum and dad had us taking swimming lessons. At 10 years old, I started training a few times a week with the Scarborough Dolphins Swim Club. I had found something I was good at and when, at my first race, I won a fifth-place ribbon I decided that I would work towards first next time! I was driven and nothing would stop me. I loved the water and continued to train, building up the number of times I went to the pool, so that by the time I was 14 I was training about ten times a week. I never complained about getting up early because I loved it. The only stipulation from my parents was that I had to make sure that my schoolwork didn't suffer or I wouldn't be allowed to go. This made me time efficient. Although I was never a 'top of the class' student, I certainly wasn't at the bottom.

Chapter 2: Unexpected Journey

At the age of 15, I remember watching the 1976 Montreal Olympics. My parents couldn't pull me away from the television; I was obsessed with watching all the televised swimming. The big thing back then was the newspaper coverage. I cut every article out that I could find and plastered them all on my bedroom wall. Canada was doing brilliantly and I re-read those articles every night in bed. That was it, I had decided; 1980, I would be there, wearing red and white, representing Canada at the Moscow Olympics. That was my goal and that was my focus.

I love the water! I honestly remember as a child believing that I should have been born a fish because I couldn't get enough of swimming. Even as a teenager training up to five hours a day, before and after school, with my hair dying and my skin so dry that all you could smell was the chlorine. I wanted to spend every waking minute training.

During the mid-to-late 70s my life was all about swimming, attending local swim meets, provincial championships and eventually nationals. I was a bit of an all-rounder, but seemed to excel at breaststroke. I loved breaststroke, but also enjoyed all the other strokes. I tended to lean towards the individual medley, as well.

My determination to make it to the 1980 Olympics continued. What I didn't count on was international politics and the Cold War. In 1980, most of the western world decided it would boycott the Moscow Olympics, which put thousands of athletes' careers on hold or at an end. In 1980, at the ripe old age of 18, my swimming career and dream came to an abrupt halt. You see, back then, 18 was considered old for a swimmer; another four years would have seen me way 'over the hill'. It was time to move on and start my life as an adult.

I decided to follow in the footsteps of my parents and become a police officer at the Metropolitan Toronto Police Force. My parents had both been officers and had met on the job back in the 1950s. I had a very exciting career working first in uniform, then undercover for four years in the prostitution and drug areas, then finally as a detective constable in the Criminal Investigation Bureau. Even while on the police force I continued to swim and eventually started to compete in triathlons. In 1985, the very first World Police and Fire Games were held in San Jose, California. I decided to head there with a small contingent of other Torontonian officers to take part. It was there in California that I met and befriended a group of Melbourne Fire Brigade officers and their wives. Over the following six years, I made several trips to Australia, to see the country and my newfound friends.

I loved my job and the people I worked with, but eventually became disillusioned. When I joined the force I had an unrealistic view of the world; I thought that I would be able to change it. But I learnt that this wasn't going to happen. It felt like no matter what we as officers did, the court system would give the accused a slap on the wrist and send them back out on the street. I can't count the number of crooks that I arrested over and over again, only to see them back on the street in a few month's time. I saw the world changing to the point where there was no respect for the uniform anymore and I wasn't sure I wanted to continue working in this line of employment.

Chapter 2: Unexpected Journey

In 1992, I decided to take a leave of absence and travel to Australia for a year. I wanted to finally see the entire country that I had fallen in love with. I had an amazing year driving 37,500 kilometres around the country. I ended up back in Melbourne in August of 1993, where I spent the last couple of months of my stay. One night, some friends took me to a local football club, where I met Russell. This was the first night of a long-lasting love affair, one that continued even when I returned home in November. Our long-distance relationship lasted eight months before Russ finally proposed. I then decided policing was no longer going to be part of my life. I packed up my belongings, said goodbye to my friends and family and moved 16,000 kilometres to Melbourne, Australia.

I love Melbourne – what an incredible place if you are a sports nut! I couldn't believe that I was able to swim in an outdoor pool in the middle of the winter! I would never have been able to do that in Canada. I became involved with the local Masters Swimming Club and with Russ at the football club where we'd met. I also got a job with Australia Post, where I slowly worked my way up the corporate ladder. Life was fantastic: I had a man who loved me; a new family that I was getting to know with step children, in-laws, nieces and nephews; a whole new set of friends; and a sport I could do all year round. What more could a person ask for?

In 1998, I felt unwell for a few months. I was extremely fatigued, regularly lost balance and had deteriorating eyesight. After some medical tests, I was told that I had Multiple Sclerosis. This is where the pigheadedness and stubbornness helped me. I was determined that MS was not going to define who I was. Yes, I had a chronic illness but, no, I wasn't going to let it control my life. This didn't happen overnight; it was a constant struggle to learn how to live with it and incorporate it into my life – not just my personal life, but my sporting and working lives as well.

2001 was my introduction to a disabled lifestyle. I had been in and out of hospital for a number of years and now had to use a wheelchair full time. It took the use of many strategies to cope and move on with my life. There were definitely extreme ups and downs, but I always seemed to pull through. During many of the down times, one of the things that kept me going was my love of the water. Sometimes my legs refused to work, but in the water I felt no different from anyone else. With the help of exercise and some medical intervention I was able to get out of the wheelchair and back on my feet, although I now used a walking stick.

Also in 2001, I had to make one of the hardest decisions of my life: leaving full-time employment. My health had deteriorated and it was time to concentrate on getting back on my feet. I had never been unemployed and wasn't sure what I was going to do with my days. Medical intervention came in the form of Botox and some intensive physiotherapy. These finally got me back on my feet after a year-long struggle.

Between trying to get my health and fitness back I started the 24 Hour Mega Swim, which is a charity event to raise money for the Go for Gold Scholarship Program run by Victoria's MS Society. This program gives people living with MS the opportunity to follow a dream. I am proud to say that the Mega Swim is still going strong and is now a huge part of MS Limited in Victoria, New South Wales and the

Chapter 2: Unexpected Journey

ACT. As of May 2015, it has raised over six million dollars. The swim now funds scholarships, a financial assistance program and assists in paying for educational programs for people learning to deal with everything relating to their diagnosis. So, without full-time employment, my time was quickly filled with looking after my body and running my charity.

In 2003, I had another health setback. In 2001, my large bowel stopped working and I had to have an ileostomy, which I coped with very well. However, in 2003 I ran into difficulties and it was decided that I would have to have my large intestine removed in the hope that the small intestine would take over. Luckily it worked, but, as my MS always worsened after surgery, I was once again back in rehab trying to relearn how to walk. Once I had accomplished that and was back out in the real world I was given the shocking news that I would have to have a full hysterectomy, as I had tumours on my ovaries and blood work suggesting possible ovarian cancer. Funnily enough, I was pretty calm about this potential threat. The diagnosis I'd received five years earlier had prepared me, and I wasn't as scared or worried as I probably should have been. I just went methodically through what needed to be done. In the end, the pathology came back good for me and I was cleared of any cancer.

Two years later, I was lucky enough to be one of the recipients of a Go for Gold Scholarship, with money raised by my own charity event. In 2005, the World Masters Games were being held in Edmonton, Alberta, Canada, and, for the first time in any Masters Games, they had Paralympic classifications in swimming and athletics. So thinking that the games would be a good idea and allow me to go back to Canada for a visit,

I got myself classified for the swimming. The games went extremely well, with me winning one silver medal and four gold medals! Without the scholarship I wouldn't have been able to afford to attend the games.

Upon arriving home, I received an email from the Australian Paralympic Development people. They had somehow heard about me and invited me to come to a Paralympic Talent Search Day at the Victorian Institute of Sport (VIS), located in Melbourne. So, in December of 2005, I attended this event and, even though I was about twenty years older, was put through the same tests as the other attendees at the same pace. I felt old that day and really didn't think that anything would come of my testing. I thought these days were for children and teens who might be stars in the future.

Just before Christmas that year I received a letter asking me to take up the sport of rowing! Rowing, of all things! I was used to being *in* the water, not on top of it. I was told that rowing was a new sport to be held at the 2008 Beijing Paralympics. Although 'adaptive' rowing, as it was called, had been part of the world rowing scene since 2002, it had never been included in the Paralympics.

After doing a 'Learn to Row' program, I threw myself into the sport. It paid off with my first national title in 2007 in the boat category of the double scull. This meant there was a chance I might compete in the 2008 Beijing Paralympics. The next year was one of growth; I had to improve at the sport and re-learn what it meant to be involved in elite sport. I was lucky enough to be granted a scholarship with the Victorian Institute of Sport. The staff there were instrumental to my success in sport.

Chapter 2: Unexpected Journey

I was named in the national team in 2008 and we had one chance of qualifying for the Beijing Paralympics. I believed my goal of representing my country at this level was finally going to come true. I was rowing in a coxed four boat with a mixed crew of two men and two women, each of whom had different disabilities. Our coxswain, the person responsible for navigating, was able-bodied. In light of these developments, I planned my year around going to Beijing.

Unfortunately, we failed to qualify for the Paralympics that year. The devastation I felt was incredible. I hadn't even considered that we could fail in our attempt. After finishing our race and reaching the dock, I had to be lifted out of the boat as my legs had nothing left in them. I lied on the dock and cried – thank God for dark sunglasses! At this point, I figured it wasn't meant to be. I was 47 years old and another four years of training and anticipation seemed impossible. I posted a blog informing everyone we hadn't succeeded, apologised to all our supporters and decided (at the spur of the moment) that I wouldn't continue. Right away, my sister sent me a message asking why. She said to just take it a minute, an hour, a day, a week, a month and a year at a time. What a novel idea; never say never!

I continued to row and, with a slightly different crew, made the national team once more in 2009. We were named part of the team to travel to Poland for the World Rowing Championships that year. We certainly weren't given any hope of making it into the finals, but we had different ideas, making the final and coming sixth. We had the worst row we had ever had! I felt very deflated after the race – until it finally sunk in that we were sixth in the world! Not bad for a group of rowers who lived thousands of kilometres away from each other and didn't have much training together. Needless to say, we all truly believed that this was our first step towards the 2012 London Paralympics. Unfortunately, towards the end of 2010, we were overlooked for inclusion in the team for the World Championships due to internal politics within the sport. I knew that I had to make some decisions about what to do in the future. Should I keep rowing, trying to change the minds of the Powers That Be within Rowing Australia; row as a Masters rower; or try something different? I never completely gave up on the idea that I could be in London in 2012, but I wasn't sure in what capacity.

In early 2011, I decided to switch sports to cycling. I had found out that there was a category for trikes and, as MS had robbed me of my balance, I had been cross-training by riding a trike. I was talked into going to the Australian National Para-Cycling Championships in April of that year by one of the other rowers, Alex Green, who had been in my crew and had switched to cycling. I knew absolutely nothing about cycling, or how to race, but went to Queensland just to take part. I was astounded when the head coach of Australian Para-cycling, Peter Day, came up to me and told me that I had just done the qualifying speed for the national team in the T2 category.[1] I didn't even know what that qualifying speed meant! I certainly had a lot of learning to do.

This change of sport was definitely a step in the right direction and, as I continued to learn about cycling and

---

[1] There are several different categories in Para-cycling, depending on whether you are on a trike, bike or hand cycle. In the trike category, there are two levels: T1 and T2, with the T2 category being more able-bodied. This was the category I fit into.

Chapter 2: Unexpected Journey

found a coach to help me out, I continued to improve and surprise myself. In 2011, I headed to my first World Para-Cycling Championships in Denmark believing that I was going to win. I had constantly been told I was the fastest T2 woman they had ever seen. Funnily enough, a Canadian girl was told the exact same thing. The problem was she was the fastest, so when I came second in the time trial I was devastated! People were coming up to me and congratulating me on my silver medal and I wasn't happy!

It took me a good half a day to realise that what I had done was astonishing; after only a few months of proper cycle training, I was second in the world! So I had to re-think the next race, which was the road race, and when I came second again I was very happy. I could have made excuses as to why I was second – my trike weighed in at 22 kgs, I weighed in at 84 kgs – but the truth is I needed to get fitter and stronger. With my coaching staff promising me a new trike if I got stronger and fitter, I embarked on a serious lifestyle change. Boy, did that make a difference!

Making the team for London 2012 was the ultimate goal and I was going to do whatever I could to get there. After months of watching what I was putting in my mouth and putting in the hard yards during training, I was presented with a trike that weighed 14 kgs. I was now down to 72 kgs, which gave me a total weight loss of 20 kgs. I felt like I was flying!

At the end of May 2012, I was officially on Australia's cycling team for London. Unfortunately, it wasn't all smooth sailing, as my spot on the team was challenged by another rider. Luckily for me that challenge was thrown out and my dream of representing my country came true. It may have been a different country, it may have been a different sport, but I had made it because I was willing to change and take a chance.

Winning a gold medal wasn't the success to me; it was actually making the team and doing the best that I could possibly do. I finished that time trial and had nothing more to give. I could have come last and would have still been successful. The gold medal just topped it all off!

So where to from a gold medal? After London, I had to sit down and decide what was next. I was not yet a world champion, so made this my goal for 2013. My training intensified and, although I was getting older, I was still young in the sport of professional cycling, so believed I could continue to improve. I was able to prove this with wins not only at the third World Cup that year, but also the 2013 World Championships, becoming World Champion in the time trial and road race. These races were more satisfying than my Paralympic races because my main competitor from Canada didn't race in London due to injury. There was always a little niggle in the back of my mind … If she had been there, would I have won? So to win both races with her there, and on her home soil, was extremely satisfying.

In 1980, if someone had told me that my dream of going to the Olympics – let alone the Paralympics – would come true thirty-two years later I would have thought they were nuts. I have been on an Unexpected Journey and one I believe can continue in any direction I want to take it. I am hoping that this book will help you to overcome adversity and accept change as part of your life, to realise that change will happen even if we don't want it to, but that it can be a good thing. By reading this book, you will learn that you can overcome the fear of change through persistence, facing your fears, moving past the hurdles, pushing past your comfort zone, learning from past lessons, focusing on the present and eventually celebrating success.

Chapter 3:
Change Happens

There are three things in life that are certain: death, which none of us want to see; taxes, which none of us like to pay; and change, which most of us dislike. But change happens every single day of our lives, from the little things like a change in our schedule or roadwork-related changes of direction while driving, to the bigger things like a change of career, a change of marital status or the onset of an illness.

Some of these changes sound very bad, but you can always find some benefits no matter what that change is.

Change triggers progress. You should look beyond the actual change to see how it can assist you in the future. When change occurs it is important to accept that it has happened, believe in yourself and your abilities, and move on. You may face obstacles along the way, but each stumble will help you change the way you tackle the problem. Your progress will demonstrate that change can work to your advantage. All small changes eventually become big!

Change can give you opportunities you never thought you would have. I always ask groups I'm speaking to what they'd attempt to do if they knew they could not fail. Unfortunately, as we age we stop trying new things because we fear we will look silly or won't be good at it. I see this in children now; they are too scared to get involved when they feel they won't be good at something, so they miss great opportunities to try new things. I say try something new each week to get used to change on a small scale. You never know what trying it might do for you.

> 'If you change the way you look at things, the things you look at change.'
> – **Wayne Dyer**

Change makes you re-evaluate your life. Are you on the right path? Is there something else you should be doing? At times, we become so set in our ways that we become stuck in a rut. If we take the time to look at things differently, we are able to move forward and let that change become the norm.

With change comes education. It is so important to be constantly learning. Changes in our lives help us learn, grow and progress. Whether it is learning a new job or learning that you have the power to do anything you choose to do. With learning, we can sometimes become frustrated because we live in an immediate society. Good changes can take time; it's all about baby steps and not expecting to be an expert overnight. Growing up, we take time to learn. It's only as adults that the instant gratification is required. We need to slow down and take time to learn how to make the changes in our lives to become successful.

Last but not least: change gives us new beginnings. I believe every day is a new beginning and that the changes that await us can be incredible. Although it may be difficult to believe this at the time of the change, it is important to take a moment during the day to think at least one positive thought. Accepting change can be as easy as changing our thought patterns. We should believe in ourselves and our abilities.

Without change, we become motionless. Without motion,

we may never progress or reach any goals we have set for ourselves. An effective change requires trust and the willingness to accept mistakes or even failure.

> 'To improve is to change; to be perfect is to change often.'
> **– Winston Churchill**

This chapter is about accepting that things don't always stay the same. We must become accepting, creative and adept at confronting challenges that are thrown our way. We can learn to deal with change in many ways. For example, we may learn through life experience, with the help of others (such as mentors) and through controlled situations, such as practicing trying something before you do it publicly.

At the start of my adult working life I joined the Toronto Police Force and was taught from the start that things could change in an instant. When you are on the street as a uniformed officer, you are constantly subjected to change – usually not the good kind. Domestic violence calls were the most difficult to answer. You could arrive on the scene of the call and have two people raging at one another. When stepping in to put a stop to it you had to be wary of both parties. At times, if you arrested one party the other would turn on you, even though moments earlier they had been at each others' throats!

During training, in order to learn how to deal with sudden change, we were put into controlled situations where we were given scenarios similar to the aforementioned. This way, we learnt how to deal with immediate changes without the risk of getting hurt. Although it was just a simulation, it gave us the ability to believe in ourselves so that we would be able to handle a real situation when the time came.

This is something that you may want to do yourself if you are scared of change. Make a change in a controlled situation, where you won't have the fear of failing. Remember: through failure, we learn what will and what won't work, which makes it easier to accept change. I believe that change is all about re-wiring our brain to accept that things will not always stay the same.

Throughout my life I experienced several major changes. Although some were extremely scary, I have come out the other side with a whole new way of looking at things. The biggest change occurred on the 23rd of April 1998 at 2.15 pm. It's funny how we remember days and times, although I suppose it would be hard not to: this day changed my life forever. A few months earlier, I'd competed at the Australian Masters Swimming Championships, which were held in Hobart, Tasmania. I thought I was in pretty good shape and anticipated some fast swims. Unfortunately, I swam like a rock and couldn't understand why. It had been about 40 degrees Celsius that week, which was highly unusual for Hobart. I was very uncomfortable; even the temperature in the pool area had soared higher than 40. I felt lethargic and thought I was coming down with the flu. When I got home, I couldn't pull myself out of bed. When I did, my balance was all over the place. Then my eyesight did funny things: I had double vision and it felt like my eyeballs were shaking from side to side. I'm sure my husband thought I was nuts when I asked him to look at my eyes moving. From his side, they were still, but to me they were shaking! My doctor thought I had an inner-ear infection, but nothing we tried

Chapter 3: Change Happens

stopped these symptoms. I even had a field vision test at the local optometrist. It turned out I wasn't seeing anything in my peripheral vision. She asked for my doctor's name and phone number, explaining that maybe this virus had spread to the optic nerve. After her conversation with my doctor, he referred me to a neurologist, where I received a number of tests. Little did I know that the optometrist had told my doctor that I had Optic Neuritis, which was a symptom of Multiple Sclerosis.

So on April 23rd I headed back to get the results. This was the day the neurologist, a so-called medical professional, told me that I indeed had Multiple Sclerosis. My symptoms had been gone for about a week and, as I had accepted my GP's diagnosis of a virus, I told Russ not to come with me to my appointment. I figured there was nothing to worry about and headed to the neurologist's office in good spirits.

I was called into the inner sanctum of the specialist's office. He ushered me into a chair, seemingly in a hurry. I thought *this must be good news! He's in a real hurry and I'm probably wasting his time.* As I sat down, he took a large envelope from his desk, pulled out a number of large negatives and held them to the light on his ceiling.

'You have Multiple Sclerosis,' he said. 'Basically, life as you know it is over. I would suggest you go home and put your affairs in order before you become incapacitated.'

It was like being hit with a brick!

'What?' I replied.

'You heard me: you have Multiple Sclerosis.' He said this matter-of-factly, then went on without a breath. 'Now, this means you will have to quit work. You will have to go on a number of drugs and won't be doing any of this silly sport stuff again. I certainly don't have time for you as a patient; I already deal with enough people with MS, so you'll have to go back to your own GP.'

He stood as he was putting the film back into the envelope and walked to the door.

'Hurry up,' he said, opening the door. 'I have patients waiting.'

As I stood, my entire world seemed to go into slow motion. This couldn't be happening. I approached the door and he thrust the envelope with my unknown future towards me. The only thing I wanted to do was stick it where the sun doesn't shine and scream that he was wrong! His last words to me were to see his secretary on the way out. I thought *you have got to be kidding!* As I headed down the hallway, I walked straight past his secretary's office. As I opened the door, the last thing I heard was 'Mrs Cooke! Mrs Cooke!' And, with that, I stepped outside into a completely new world.

To this day, I don't remember driving home. Had I not been the person I am, it could have very well been the last day of my life. I know I drove home, but have no idea what route I took or how I made it there. The first thing I remember is sitting at home with my head in my hands, crying. My 6-month-old puppy then put her head on my lap and started to whimper, which snapped me out of my tears. I then made

Chapter 3: Change Happens

decisions that I thought would benefit myself and Russ – that is, until he arrived home.

I told him what had happened at the appointment and about the decisions I had made. Since I was going to be 'incapacitated', I decided I would give Russ the house we had just purchased. I would give him a divorce and go home to Canada, where my family could look after me. Russ is ten years older than me and I wasn't sure how he would cope looking after me once I became 'incapacitated'. We had only been married for three years, so I had figured it was better to let Russ go his own way now than wait until it all got too hard.

I am very lucky Russ was more level-headed than me at that point. A true bush-boy Aussie, he bluntly told me I was a 'fucking idiot', and reminded me that we didn't know anything about this disease, that *we* had it – him and I – and would deal with whatever was going to happen. I decided I had to learn more about this disease so I could deal with what might happen in the future. I needed to go to the experts for the information that I so desperately needed.

I look back on this change in my life in a whole new light now. It certainly made me re-evaluate where I was headed and where I wanted it to go. Life was all about climbing the corporate ladder and trying to make as much money as possible, to build what I thought was a better lifestyle. This diagnosis made me think about the direction I was headed in. What was so great about stressing over work and making money if I wasn't healthy enough to enjoy it?

I also learned that it's not a smart move to make radical

decisions in a very emotional state. I needed to go through a type of grieving process to accept that life was not going to be the same anymore. It was not necessarily going to be worse, just different. Accepting this change certainly didn't happen overnight. At first, I doubted my diagnosis because my symptoms had gone. However, my inner voice told me what I knew to be true. That's when I realised I needed to learn more about MS, how to accept a chronic illness and how to continue to live my life.

I can honestly say I wouldn't change my diagnosis, as it has made me who I am and given me opportunities that I never would have had without MS. I like who I am now more than the person I was before my diagnosis. This major change, which I thought was the end of my world, has been the catalyst to trigger progress, help me attain goals and introduce opportunities I never knew existed.

It wasn't until years later that I learnt another way to cope with change and that was through a friend of mine, Warren MacDonald. Warren had lost both his legs in an accident while camping and hiking on Queensland's Hinchenbrook Island. Warren taught me it's not about what you see, but how you see it. When first diagnosed, I was adamant that I would never use a walking stick or wheelchair. I thought doing so would mean I had given in to this disease. I didn't want MS to dictate my life. But, by changing the way I saw things, I realised that using aids when necessary would give me freedom to get on with life. In 2001, I needed to use a wheelchair. By changing my perspective, I stopped worrying whether I had succumbed to my MS and just changed the way I did things. The wheelchair was giving me the freedom to get out of the house, to socialise and to continue to live my life.

Chapter 3: Change Happens

What an amazing world this would be if we could all reassess how we see things. We all experience changes to our life plan, but we have to remember that the actual changes aren't important; the way we deal with them or 'how we see them' is what matters. We can decide to curl up and die or we can embrace them. Some of the changes we face will be good and some will be bad. Life won't always be fair. How we deal with those changes is what will make the difference.

We must all decide if change will be a problem or an opportunity. Is it a negative or a positive, a limitation or a challenge? How we view our surroundings is up to us. I tend to lean towards the opportunities, the positives and the challenges.

Positive reinforcement is one of the keys to accepting change, but there will always be people with concerns or objections. I am sure there are people who would say to me:

'But what if the change is bad?'

Of course there will be changes that seem bad, but I believe that there is always some good in any change. Even though I was diagnosed with a progressive chronic illness – which, in my books, is bad – there was eventual good that came from that diagnosis. It gave me opportunities to represent my adopted country at an international level in two sports: rowing and cycling. It gave me the opportunity to become an ambassador for MS Australia, to help educate, advocate and motivate. It gave me the chance to introduce and expand my charity event, the 24 Hour Mega Swim, which has raised over $6 million to assist people living with MS in the form of scholarships, financial assistance and education. So, even though that diagnosis was a 'bad' change for me, good has come from it.

What if You Don't Want to Change?
I think change is inevitable in life. We experience change every single day. If we didn't have change, life would be very boring, unexciting and predictable. Again, it is about reinforcing positive thinking into situations. It may not happen right away, but eventually it will.

What if the Change Means There are No More Options?
I believe there is always an option of some sort. You just have to look in different directions, look outside the square. There is a saying that when one door closes another one opens. I like to tell people that, sure, the door will be there, but most of the time you'll have to look for it and sometimes even force it open.

When my rowing dream was at a crossroads and I wasn't sure what was going to happen with our crew, I started looking for another avenue to fulfil my dream of going to the Paralympics. When the door to cycling presented itself, it was up to me to grab it and open up the possibilities. Thankfully, I did because it proved to me that dreams really do come true!

I don't believe we can accept change without working on it; it is a never-ending process. To do this on a daily basis, we must try something new each day. This can be as small as smiling at a stranger or just saying 'G'day'. Another thing you could try if you're experiencing change in your life is to write a sentence outlining the positive outcomes of the change. Post it somewhere where you will see it each day.

Chapter 3: Change Happens

This will reprogram our brains to think positively about change. Then, in a week, add another positive outcome to the list. You will eventually have a list of positive outcomes that demonstrate that the change is good.

Each morning, I wake up and think positively about the day ahead. I think about what amazing changes the day may bring. Change is here to stay, so learn to embrace it.

Chapter 4:
Finding Courage

Courage and fear go hand in hand. We all face fear, but finding the courage to reach for our goals comes from within. Fulfilment and success doesn't come from staying within your comfort zone. You have to use that fear to make an impact.

Most of us facing change are fearful of what that might bring. Fortunately, this chapter is about facing your fears, and believing in yourself and your abilities. It's about believing that every experience – good or bad – will help build your strength, confidence and courage. All of us have some fear of change; the familiar is more comforting and stable than what might be. The uncertainty of how change will affect us can be scary.

Although we all fear change, some of us also fear success. For those people, finding the courage to push through can be daunting. Success can be more complex than failure; it is more comfortable not being successful and staying where you are. Psychologist Matina Horner first diagnosed this fear of success in the early 1970s. We tend to doubt ourselves, but it is important to realise that this is a natural part of stepping out of comfort zones. Use fear as your fuel to move forward and let the courage you find ensure success. It is important to find out what is holding you back from making changes. What is the root of your fear and how can you find the courage to confront it head on? It will be uncomfortable to face that fear because it is unfamiliar, but let this discomfort energise you.

Fear can be your friend and the catalyst to finding courage, but too much can be debilitating. It is important that fear doesn't control you, but without it we wouldn't have courage. You have to look at what that fear is; identify what is causing the fear and whether it is a real, relevant or perceived fear. Most of the time the fear that we face isn't reasonable and you should stop and ask yourself if this is something you will worry about in a year's time. Most of the time you will find that, no, it isn't a reasonable fear and you will find the courage to move forward and take steps towards a positive outcome. If we don't move forward it is possible we will miss an amazing experience. We fear change in business because we have comfortable routines. However, it's important to embrace change because there are often better ways of doing things.

The study of psychology teaches us that the capacity to fear is part of human nature, but that people develop fears as the result of learning. The older we get, the more fear we find. Think back to when we were children and how we would try anything; we seemed invincible. As we age, we know that we aren't invincible, so those fears start to invade our life. We have conditioned ourselves to remember that things can and sometimes do go wrong. We tend to be cautious and stay within our comfort zone, but this can leave us stuck in a rut, unable to move forward.

Use your fear not just to help clarify your goals, but to identify what you are fearful of. This will ensure you reach your goals in a timely fashion. If you can identify the fears keeping you from your goals, you can set a plan to reach those goals. There have been a number of times in my life when I have had to find courage to accomplish a goal.

Chapter 4: Finding Courage

I grew up in a family full of police officers. Growing up, it seemed to me my dad had been a policeman forever. He actually met my mum on the force. My grandfather had been a policeman as well, as had his brother and a couple of my dad's cousins. But Dad was different from the rest. He rose steadily through the ranks. As a young child, I decided I would never be a police officer because I could never be as good as my dad.

However, at the ripe old age of 18, I decided to get a job as a clerk on the force. It didn't stop there. After about six months of working in the Records Information Bureau, where we did checks on people and wrote up the major incidents for press releases, I decided I would become a police officer as well. I didn't know if I could ever live up to the kind of cop my dad was, but I thought I'd give it a shot.

I had a great career and thought it would continue for the rest of my working life. I was driven to do the best I could and, after about five years in uniform, I moved to the Morality Bureau, working in an undercover capacity. The Morality Bureau dealt with prostitution, drugs and gambling, and I worked there for about four years. It was an incredible time; I was young and felt like I had the world at my feet. At first, I spent most of my time working on prostitution, dealing with not only runaways who had been taken in by pimps, but by posing as a runaway to see if they would try to get me to work the street. We also targeted the other side of prostitution: the customers. This could be another whole book, as there was always controversy about how to tackle the oldest profession in the world!

I then moved into the drug area, taking part not only in

the small projects of street-level drug trades and in public housing, but in bigger projects that could last a couple of months. I certainly learned that there was a lot going on in the city of Toronto that I never thought would have ever happened.

I then moved on to the Criminal Investigation Branch in one of the downtown Toronto stations, 14 Division. This certainly opened my eyes to the world around me. I had some amazing partners who taught me a lot. By the start of 1992, I was beginning to question if being a police officer was what I wanted to do. I had gone into the job thinking I could change the world and had learnt over the years that this certainly wasn't going to happen on my own or with others for that matter. I had come into the job with an innocent outlook on life and, fourteen years later, now had a cynical, hardened outlook.

As a police officer, you only really hang around with work colleagues. This is due to shift work and the emotional stuff you are forced to deal with. It is easier to talk to work colleagues; family and friends can never comprehend what you deal with on a daily basis. I felt that I needed to get away from this and really decide on my own if I wanted to continue with this career. I was afraid all I could be was a cop, that I had nothing else to offer in any other profession and that I would become someone who hated life. So I took a leave of absence for a year in November 1992 and travelled to Australia. It took me a good six months to get out of 'cop' mode and really learn who I was again as an individual. It was tough. I was scared to leave my comfort zone and had only a few friends in Australia to rely on. I left family, friends and my career (with no pay for a year), but it was a good thing to do.

Chapter 4: Finding Courage

I had an amazing year meeting people I never would have associated with in the past because of my profession and tried many new things that pushed me out of my comfort zone. I met my future husband Russ towards the end of this year off. Although I had to go back to work at the end of November in 1993, we continued our relationship through letters, phone calls and travel. I threw myself back into policing with a stint in uniform. It was my job to train the new police officers who were coming into the job.

During a quick trip to Melbourne in June of 1994, Russ proposed and, after coming home to let my family and friends know, it was time to make a decision: would I leave my job and country to live in Australia, or would Russ move to Canada? To me, it was a no-brainer. Russ had children to consider and I would never have asked him to leave them. Unfortunately, as easy as I thought it would be to leave my career and life, I struggled! Even after a year away from police work, and even though I knew it wasn't what I wanted to do with the rest of my life, I struggled to put a timeframe on how long I should continue this career.

When I joined the force, I thought I'd continue in this career for my entire life. That was what my family had done; it was what was expected. My colleagues were like family and, going through Police College, the sentiment that this is a lifelong career path is practically brainwashed into you. I honestly believed it was all I could do, so changing careers was a daunting aspect of my move to Australia. Having the year off had taught me there was a whole world out there beyond policing, but not knowing what I would do for work was scary.

After fourteen years, I handed in my police gear and tried to prepare for a whole new life! There were going-away parties and dinners with friends and family, but I don't think it truly hit me until I was sitting on the plane on the Toronto runway, waiting for takeoff: I was making the biggest change of my life and heading to a new country and a new life.

As the plane took off, I started to cry. I honestly don't know if they were tears of fear or joy. I was scared, but excited at the same time. It took a lot of courage to decide to leave behind everything I knew, everything I had, everything that was comfortable to me. I had no idea what kind of life I was embarking on; all I knew was a man who loved me was waiting for me.

Thinking back now, I see that if I hadn't taken that leap of faith, I would never have realised the amount of possibilities I have. It has been a wonderful life and whole new way of living. There have obviously been challenges, but the rewards that come with finding the courage to get through those challenges have been enormous. Finding that courage has also taught me that, thanks to my prior police work, I possess many skills I never realised I had. Finding a job was not difficult. Policing had given me patience and time management, managerial and communication skills. I wasn't scared to take a 'bottom-rung' job and work my way up, which is what I did, gaining employment with Australia Post.

Finding courage has been critical in my life – not only because I moved halfway around the world and have had to deal with my Multiple Sclerosis diagnosis, but also because of my sporting life.

Chapter 4: Finding Courage

I was a rower before I started cycling. I found out that the coach I had at the time had been lying to me and done things behind my back. Similar to my experiences at Police College, I'd been brainwashed to believe he was the only one who could coach me to the top level. No matter what I did I couldn't get myself to dump him as a coach and go with someone else. This caused many psychological problems for me and I was eventually forced to look for assistance, which came in the form of a sports psychologist.

Most people are scared to honestly talk about their problems. To be honest, I was definitely one of those people who thought they could handle everything on their own. However, I couldn't see a way out of this situation on my own. I worked with this sports psychologist for several sessions. She showed me how to end my association with this coach. There were a number of issues, but I think the biggest fear was the question of who would coach me, if not him. Fortunately, my sports psychologist made me see that courage would come from finding someone who could properly coach me.

I know that seems simple, but when you are in the middle of a situation you are emotionally tied to the problem. Sometimes, you can't or won't see the simple answers that are in front of you. This psychologist taught me to put my fear to good use. She taught me that the beginning of courage always feels like fear, but that courage will grow if you focus on the potential outcome of your situation. I was then able to extricate myself from that bad situation, which, in turn, made me a much stronger person and taught me that I could do the same thing in the future, no matter the challenge.

> 'I learned that courage was not the absence of fear, but the triumph over it. The brave man is not he who does not feel afraid, but he who conquers that fear.'
> **– Nelson Mandela**

Finding courage isn't just about those big changes in your life; it's about the little ones as well. The more I got into cycling, the more I realised I had fears that were specific to the sport, such as how to race the road race. Ultimately, this was a fear of the unknown. I didn't yet have the knowledge to race it; I didn't understand the tactics involved. I am fine with time trials, as it is simply you against the clock, but add in additional elements, like other riders, and I became fearful. I had butterflies in my stomach and nervousness on the start line.

In the beginning, I raced the road race like it was a time trial, hoping for the best. But as more and more women come into the trike category, it became apparent that I would need to overcome my fear of tactics and learn what to do. But how would I learn this?

A great way to find courage is to speak with others who have been there before you. I have spoken to coaches (and not just my own), to other riders within the Para community and to able-bodied riders to gain perspective on what they do. I have learned from my mistakes and from my fear of trying something different. I have now proven to myself that persistence and forward momentum will eventually make those possibilities realities.

I'm still not completely comfortable with the tactics of road racing, but I am certainly willing to work on the little things that will improve my competency. I have learned that the butterflies and nervousness can help me in those races. I have also learned what my strengths and weaknesses are within my races, and that by working on my weaknesses I will find the courage to take on even bigger problems should they arise. It's about baby steps. Tackle one problem at a time and, in no time at all, I won't remember I was once scared of competing in a road race.

I am sure there are people out there who've thought my goals were unrealistic, especially making it to a Paralympic games at my age. And I am sure there are people who think their own goals are unrealistic, so are fearful of voicing them. We should not believe any goals are unrealistic, nor should we fear attaining them. The best thing to do is break that final goal into smaller steps, so that each small achievement is celebrated. Little goals along the way create momentum and it is truly amazing when we finally realise that we have attained our major goal.

Some people may question whether they are good enough, but this is just fear and doubt talking. By just taking those baby steps or small actions, those fears and doubts will start to fade. If you are still having trouble, shift your focus and find another way to accomplish what you set out to do. Keeping on a positive course will feed your confidence and you will find yourself moving forward. As long as you are attempting to move forward, your fear will diminish. You will find the courage to accomplish what you set out to do and leave your doubts behind.

We all have the choice to bring our dreams to life. We can

choose the path we follow and decide whether we want to live in fear or find the courage to push through. I like to call this the three C's of life. You must have Courage and take a Chance, or you will never get through the Change. It is important to listen to your fears. Choose to take that chance and you will move forward within that change.

It is important to have commitment and direction.

> 'Efforts and courage are not enough without purpose and direction.'
> – **John F Kennedy**

Here are some helpful ways to find courage:

- Commit your goal to paper. It will make it real. Post it somewhere you will see it everyday and it will clarify exactly what you want. Knowing what you want will motivate you to take action and will help you measure your progress. Don't worry about the fear and resistance you may feel; celebrate each time you achieve one of your baby steps and record it on your goal paper.

- Find a favourite quote about courage. Find one you really believe in, type it out and, again, post it in a conspicuous place where you will see it all the time. Remember, only positive thoughts will bring positive achievements and you can actually teach yourself to be courageous. It is like telling yourself something positive each day, except that someone else has come up with the quote.

- Try something new. There is an anonymous quote that says 'To get something you never had, you have to do something you never did.' There are different kinds of courage for different scenarios, so it is important to try something new in all aspects of your life. Each month, try something that will push you out of your comfort zone. Even little things can help lessen your fear and, eventually, this will help build your confidence so that you can believe in yourself and trust your abilities. This could be what you need to learn to trust and have faith in yourself. A fear of trying something new is a good sign. It means you are human and are truly in the moment and getting past your comfort zone.

Chapter 5:
Jumping Hurdles

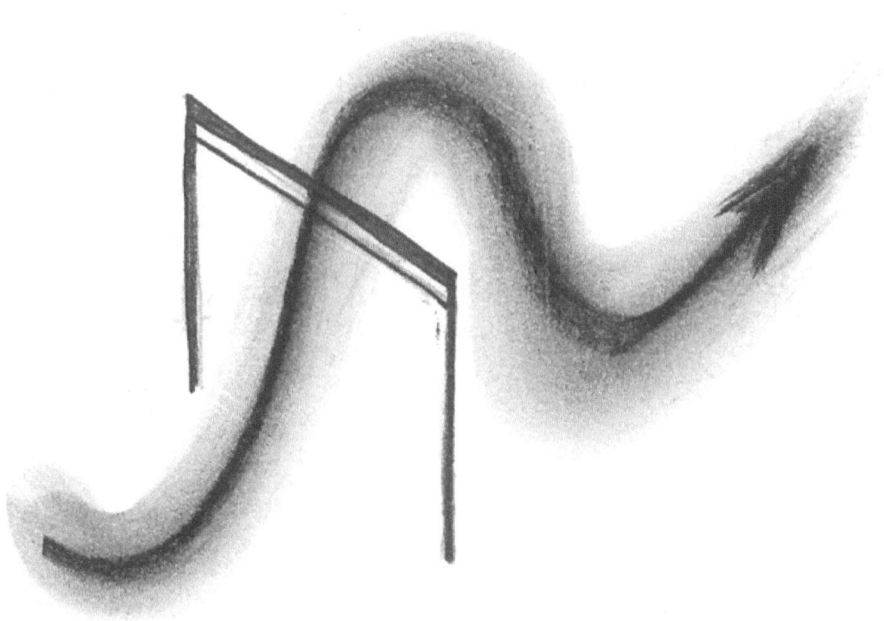

No matter what our plans or goals are, we will always face challenges. We must identify what those challenges will be if we hope to overcome them. Will they be environmental, personal or social obstacles? Are they controllable or out of your control? We have to remember that we can only control the controllable!

It is important to understand that there are always ways around obstacles. Sometimes it's about thinking outside the box and realising that hurdles and obstacles can be good for us. If jumping hurdles were easy, everyone would be reaching their goals immediately and not appreciating the joy of the journey. If we had no challenges, life would be pretty boring.

Sometimes those obstacles in front of us are only there because we don't believe in our own abilities. Fortunately, those obstacles can make you more determined to reach your goals. Although constantly being challenged is frustrating, that frustration will help you look at options and ways around the obstacle you face.

> 'If you can't believe in miracles, then believe in yourself. When you want something bad enough, let that drive push you to make it happen. Sometimes you'll run into brick walls that are put there to test you. Find a way around them and stay focused on your dream. Where there's a will, there's a way.'
> **– Unknown**

Determination will give you a sense of self-worth and help you become more focused, creative and disciplined. In the end, reaching your goal will feel like an accomplishment. This creativeness will help you alter your perception and behaviour, and will help turn the obstacle into a solvable stepping stone.

It is important when faced with an obstacle to take a step back. Don't let the emotion of the problem make you react in the wrong way. Take a deep breath or count to ten before you do something that may make the obstacle worse. Emotional responses to obstacles can have adverse reactions. Step back and look at the problem from someone else's perspective. You must determine what the best course of action will be and assess the obstacles in your way.

If you are truly committed to reaching your goal you will find the determination within you to jump the hurdles that are blocking your path. Determination involves persevering towards a difficult goal in spite of obstacles. If we had no obstacles in our lives we would never grow or find new opportunities. These obstacles help us alter our behaviour and attitudes.

As mentioned in Chapter 2, it's not what you see, but *how* you see it. Some look at the obstacles and hurdles they encounter as evidence of failure, but it's better to see them as challenges that will make each accomplishment that much sweeter.

One way of overcoming obstacles is to have an amazing team around you. Most of the sports that I have been involved with have, for the most part, been individual sports. However, that doesn't mean I do everything on my own. I wouldn't be able to train or compete the way I do without an amazing team around me. If you are striving towards a goal, it is important to have people on your team who can help you get over the hurdles you will face.

My team at home consists of my husband, Russ, who looks after my food, laundry, cleaning and shopping needs; and family and friends, whom I can bounce problems off to see if they have any better solutions. It is important to have these people around you, no matter what your goal or dream may be. They are the people who keep me grounded and level-headed. I am never scared to ask for their opinions.

The professional component of my team comprises my coaches. I have cycling, gym and sport science coaches, the latter of which tackle the intricate details of my training. It is important that they work together to put the best type of training in place for me and review what works. Because I am older than most of my competitors, we must make sure my training is right. I don't want to do too much and burn out, nor do too little and be left unprepared for a race.

Another part of the team is the medical staff, which includes massage therapists, chiropractor, physiotherapists, neurologist, GP and my nutritionist. Without their efforts, I wouldn't be still out here competing at my age. All of these team members keep me on the right path and help me over any hurdles I encounter.

These team members were so important to me on August 5th, 2012. I was taking part in a local time trial race, one month before my time trial at the 2012 London Paralympics.

It was my last racing hit before I headed overseas. I was racing on Yarra Boulevard in Kew, Victoria, a road I train on regularly and know intimately. This was a race, however, and you tend to push yourself that little bit harder during races. There is a hairpin turn on the course's downhill slope. I was only 4 kms from the finish line when disaster struck.

Now, trikes aren't known to be great on corners. Add the speed of going downhill and you have a recipe for disaster. I came into the turn too fast and, in my attempt to slow down, hit some of the raised markings on the road, which threw the trike to the side. I hit the brakes hard, thinking I was going to hit the small wall dividing the cars from bikes. Unfortunately, I hit the front break harder than the back brake and headed straight over the front of the handle bars! Luckily, I turned my head to the side and, as I went over the handle bars, raised my left arm to soften the impending blow.

Upon landing, I thought I had broken my hip and collarbone. At that instant the only thing going through my mind was *Well, that's London gone!* The road was still open to vehicular traffic and, as I tried to extricate myself from my trike, I realised that I had to get out of the middle of the road or I was in danger of being hit by a car as well!

I was eventually able to get myself up and over to the side of the road, where I was assisted by someone who knew me. I wanted to get back on the trike and finish the race; I knew I would stiffen up if I didn't. I also wanted to see if anything was broken, so figured riding would be a good test. With the help of a Good Samaritan, I gingerly got back on the trike and rode the last four kilometres, holding my left arm

Chapter 5: Jumping Hurdles

across my chest. I really don't know how I rode that last kilometre, but I did, and was helped by people at the finish. The next couple of days were a bit of a blur. Doctors at the VIS made sure nothing was broken and I had to let the head coach of Australian Para-cycling know that I had crashed. I felt that everything regarding London was up in the air. This was certainly the biggest hurdle I had ever come up against. I had many questions going through my head. *Would they still take me? Would I be able to ride?*

That is why it is so important to have a good team in place. Everyone still believed in my ability, so I was luckily still included in the team. A big hurdle was going to be taking the long-haul flight. The most important thing for me was to ensure I was comfortable for the twenty-six-hour flight. This meant upgrading out of economy. It was something I really couldn't afford, but I needed to find a way if I really wanted to achieve my goal of racing in London. I eventually headed to France, where I met up with some of the team for a training camp. The credit card took a beating, but I went in style! It was the best thing I could have done. It gave me lots of room for my body and I was pampered by the Qantas staff. Our cycling staff believed in me so much that they provided massage therapy everyday for the three weeks I was in France.

I didn't expect what happened next! Physically, I was getting better; movement was returning to my shoulder and the bruises were slowly going away. Mentally, however, I wasn't doing that great. I was scared to get back on the trike. This was a hurdle I had to overcome, and something I had never experienced before in my life. Fear was a new concept to me and a big road block. I had never been afraid of much;

I had always been one to just go out and do what I had to do. Overcoming this new fear was an interesting challenge.

I was grateful to have our mechanic Dan to ride with those first few days in France. He was the one who helped me overcome my fear that I would come off again. He didn't push me to go fast, but allowed me to ride very slowly and get used to being on the trike again. He stayed with me no matter how slow I was riding. This stumbling block could have gone two ways: it could have stopped me from competing in London, or it could cause me to draw on my positive mindset and believe in the possibilities. This crash and the limitations I felt were actually blessings in disguise. It may have slowed me down for a number of days, but it made me realise that if I could get past this little setback I could get through anything. The outcome in London – winning a gold medal in the time trial – was proof to me that I could overcome anything!

A big hurdle for me when I started rowing was getting the Powers That Be to believe as much as I did in my ability. Early in 2007, I put a call in to Rowing Australia to find out what I had to do to qualify for the Paralympics in Beijing in 2008. I was told that I would have to row at Nationals, not the following year but *that* year – 2007. Now, I had only been properly training for a couple of months because, although I had completed a rowing course in June of 2006, I had an MS relapse, so was in hospital towards the end of that year. When I was told I had to row at the 2007 Nationals in February that year, I was more than concerned! That, to me, was a huge and quick stepping stone. I found out I was able to row in a double with an able-bodied rower sitting in the bow of the boat with me stroking it. I found a rower from our club to row with me and we actually won! I couldn't believe it: I was a national champion!

In May that year, I saw that Rowing Australia was having a classification workshop in Canberra. This was to train classifiers and internationally classify rowers from Australia. I enquired by email if I should go to be classified. The response I got back was deplorable; if I had been a 17-year-old I would have likely quit the sport. The reply I received said, in no uncertain terms, that I would never be fit or good enough to make a national team. This was yet another hurdle to overcome. I was extremely angry, but instead of reacting immediately I took a couple of days to compose my response. I then sent my response to this gentleman, politely telling him what he could do with his comments. I said he had no idea who I was, or how mentally strong I was. I also sent my response to his boss, the CEOs of Rowing Australia and Rowing Victoria, and my own coach. Within a couple of days, I had an invite to classification and a rowing camp for the weekend, with all expenses paid. The following year, when I made the national team, I told this man's boss matter-of-factly that he should post my email all around the office. They had to learn never to discount anyone and he agreed. This was one major hurdle I was happy to climb over!

One of the other ways I deal with obstacles is to keep a training log. As a young swimmer in the 1970s, I was taught to keep a training log, not just for writing down my workouts, but also to write about my goals, any challenges I was facing and my eventual progress. I have continued this practice to this day and it has certainly proved invaluable. I'm able to look back and see how I have improved and how I jumped any hurdles. This practice has helped me stay motivated, persistent and taught me to keep a positive attitude.

I like to keep things practical. Looking back at my journals has helped me concentrate on short-term goals, which eventually got me to those bigger outcomes. I have always had a strong desire to succeed and looking back at how I have achieved success helps me stay positive and optimistic when I set further goals.

My training journals have always been very specific and structured. I also try to remain positive. It doesn't mean that I don't have days when negativity sneaks in, but I try not to let it linger. It also doesn't mean that everything in my journals is positive; by writing down the things that don't go right, I am able to work out how to better approach those things in the future.

Since there will always be doubts, you may feel like you are going backwards when facing obstacles. At times, you have to expect discomfort while trying to attain your goal. You have to stay positive and not give up. Watch and learn from others, but also take responsibility for working through those obstacles yourself. It may be important to re-evaluate your goals if things constantly go wrong; review and work out whether your goal is actually attainable. If you believe that it is but still face an uphill battle, you may have to work out if your behaviour is contributing to the obstacles.

There are a few ways that you can help yourself overcome any challenges:
- List potential challenges. When setting a goal, it's important to pre-empt hurdles by making a list of possible challenges and strategies to overcome them. Remember to think outside the box. The answer may be something that you would have

never thought of. This list can change during the course of working towards your goal and, as you strive towards that goal, make sure you are constantly re-evaluating those possible hurdles so you can be ready for anything.

- Trust your own intuition and gut feelings. What may work for someone else may not work for you. If facing a challenge, take instruction from your team but also listen to your intuition. There will be times you'll feel persuaded to take one course of action, but trust in yourself if you don't feel it is the right direction to go in.

- Change your thinking patterns. Instead of asking why you *can't* do something, ask yourself 'How can I overcome this hurdle?' Problems test our resolve, so it is important to use them as stepping stones to reach your goals, hopes and dreams. You will realise that most of those challenges will be very small compared to your final dream. As Muhammad Ali once said, 'Often it isn't the mountain ahead that wears you out; it's the little pebble in your shoe.'

- Reflect on past successes. Sit quietly and think about the last obstacle you faced and how you got past it. You were able to get past it, so it is up to you to believe in yourself. Self-belief is an amazing thing; it will help you see possibilities and opportunities when trying to jump hurdles. Believing in yourself will stimulate you into action and help you persist in getting over those hurdles. If you need to do positive thinking exercises then do them. Write down the things that you have achieved and the hurdles you have cleared. Once you see them in black and white your self-belief will improve.

I have achieved what I have because I have had belief in my abilities. I may have started out learning the basics of a new project, (whether that be rowing or cycling), but I have always believed in my abilities to excel and enjoy whatever I undertake. I have always been willing to move out of my comfort zone, which takes courage. But that courage comes from gritting your teeth and working through the fear that you may have. If you think positively, act positively and be positive, you can't help but succeed.

Chapter 6:
Ultimate Growth

We should never stop learning in life. Education gives us the opportunity to make better decisions. This chapter is about finding out what you are capable of. Through knowledge, the fear of the unknown is lifted, allowing us to reach goals we once thought were unattainable. A failure to learn guarantees you will become stagnant and fearful of new experiences. You have the option to move forward to achieve your goals and dreams, or stay in a perpetual motionless state.

We have all heard the phrase 'knowledge is power', but do we really know what it means? It is an important phrase to understand, as it will give us the ability to make better decisions, which can be helpful when we have goals in mind. But is knowledge really power? I honestly don't know, but the act of sharing knowledge is powerful and the experience of learning empowers us. By sharing knowledge, we can remove the fear of the unknown. With this knowledge comes more options and more paths that we can follow to attain our goals.

There are two ways of attaining this new knowledge. Firstly, we can learn it from others who have gone before us. There are certainly many people in the world who may have had similar goals and experiences to you, so it is important to learn from them. Secondly, a lot of our new knowledge comes from overcoming adversity in our own lives. We tend to learn from our mistakes. It is never easy to admit that we have made mistakes, but it is important to ensure we learn from them. We must first take responsibility for our mistakes in order to gain knowledge from them. If we constantly blame someone or something else for our mistakes we will never take the time to learn from them. Sometimes, growing up, we are made to feel that making mistakes is bad. However, without failure and mistakes, we will never become successful. Some new knowledge can only be gained by making mistakes. Every minute is an opportunity to improve, even when you are making mistakes. Making mistakes or discovering weaknesses are opportunities to improve.

With new knowledge comes personal and professional growth. This will help us find resolutions and solutions to the many challenges we may face. We don't always make the best choices in our lives, which could be because we make choices based on our own experiences. Without new knowledge, we will continue to do the same thing time and again. This new knowledge can help us make those choices more viable, which will, in turn, help us grow.

Knowledge helps us find solutions to our challenges. If you hit an obstacle, new knowledge will help you look at things differently. It can help you progress to that ultimate goal.

Knowledge will also help you expand your level of thinking. As individuals, we will never know everything. Even top elite athletes or top executives will never know everything; if they did, they would never have a purpose in life, or strive to attain anything. Life would become very boring. Fortunately, by expanding your level of thinking, you can create a whole new world of possibilities.

Chapter 6: Ultimate Growth

Knowledge makes things simpler and easier. The more you know, the more you can control and build on your skills. This will make you more attuned to reaching your goals. You will make better-educated decisions using the knowledge you have gained. But you must put that knowledge into action if you hope to move forward.

When I was diagnosed with Multiple Sclerosis, I was not given any information about the disease from the first neurologist I saw. All I was given were blunt comments like 'go home and put your affairs in order' and 'you'll never do that sport stuff again', which stopped me in my tracks. My life *was* sport – always had been – so how was I going to cope with an incapacitated body and no sport in my life? I was very lucky to have an amazing general practitioner, Dr Jeff, who told me that we needed information about MS to make informed decisions.

Dr Jeff took it upon himself to get a huge packet of information not just for Russ and I, but also for himself. He told me when he was a young doctor going through training he had to learn so much about so many diseases that he was only able to spend about twenty minutes learning about MS. So he wanted to learn along with us, so that he'd be able to help as much as possible. After reading all the information I was sent, I decided that no one was going to tell me how to live or how my life would turn out. To be honest, I was most likely in some denial about the diagnosis because all of my symptoms had gone. I wondered why anyone would suggest I would have to give up any parts of my life. I was pigheaded, stubborn and believed I could conquer this disease. So I just kept doing what I had been doing in life, without thinking about any consequences of the disease. Even though I had received information about this disease, I refused to consider it and change the way I was doing things.

Reality quickly hit when symptoms began appearing. I tried to keep doing what I was doing and ended up in hospital a number of times each year, with my symptoms worsening. From my own mistakes, I realised I had to learn how to incorporate MS management into my life. I had to gain the knowledge to better manage my symptoms while continuing to do sport. I had to stop fighting the MS and learn to live with it, and I had to try to do this in a positive way. Some incredible people helped me with this journey of knowledge.

With the help of staff from MS Australia, information sessions and working with my swim coach at the time, I was able to continue swimming and even compete as a swimmer with a disability. I made sure that I got involved with programs run by MS Australia to meet other people with MS and see how they dealt with their similar symptoms. But I also realised that the power of positive thinking was going to be another important tool for me to use. I'm not saying that every waking moment is filled with positive thoughts, but I did learn that being positive certainly helps a situation. I've learnt that the power of positive thinking is important for success.

It was through my involvement with swimming that I came to the attention of the Australian Paralympic Committee and, in late 2005, I was invited to a talent search day. During this event, I learned about a number of different sports that I could get involved with. A few weeks later, I received a letter asking me to take up the sport of rowing, as it was a new event at the 2008 Beijing Paralympics. This is when the knowledge of positive thinking kicked in. I decided I wanted to learn everything possible about the sport of rowing and incorporate this knowledge into my life.

I realised that no matter how disabled I became I could always take part in rowing because of the different types of boats that could be used. I contacted local clubs and eventually took a 'Learn to Row' course. I then started with the club and began training regularly. However, because MS is such a difficult disease to understand and deal with, training knowledge was limited; it was more a case of trying different things to see what worked. It was like learning on the job and I constantly tried to impart the knowledge I was gaining on coaches who came into my life.

We certainly learnt from the number of mistakes I made. Because of my MS-related balance problems, I had to learn to row in a single scull, which was interesting. I ended up in the Yarra River on a number of occasions. I eventually worked out how to balance by focusing on a single point at the stern of the boat. Then there was the difficult problem of navigating the river as it wound its way upstream. This was challenging because I lost balance whenever I had to turn my head from side to side. Fortunately, I was able to learn from other rowers about points that I could look at to ensure my stern lined up with them as we followed the bends of the river. This way, I didn't have to turn my head. My rowing progressed until I was able to compete and do pretty well. But I was hungry for more knowledge on the sport, so took it upon myself to take a coaching course. To me, the more I learned about the sport, the better chance I had of taking it to a higher level.

One of my favourite quotes is:

> 'If you are not continually updating your knowledge, you will be left behind. You must always be looking for a better way to do something, for the knowledge that will make you more effective. Because you can be sure that your competition is doing just that.'
> – Ralph Marston, GreatDay.com

I found it was important to remain positive about learning to row. It was certainly frustrating at times. Sometimes, others had negative reactions towards my rowing goals. I really had to ignore what those people were saying or trying to do. As I mentioned before, there were people within the sport who, at times, told me I would never be good enough, or that I was getting too old for the sport. Because of this, it was a constant struggle to remain positive and push towards my goal. The more I learnt about my capabilities, the more I wanted to prove those people wrong.

A similar thing happened when I wanted to get a bike to ride, just back and forth to rowing training. Knowing that my balance was bad and that I would fall over on two wheels, I did some research into three-wheeled vehicles. The first trike I found weighed about 40 kgs, so I wanted something that was at least a little lighter. When I got a trike I could train on and potentially race, I realised I needed to learn more about how to ride a trike. Unfortunately, I couldn't find anyone in Australia to teach me much about it, so most of my knowledge came from trial and error. Since then, I have been able to find people across the world who I can call upon to answer any questions I have. The best thing about gaining this knowledge is that now I can pass it on to others who are now riding trikes in Australia.

Chapter 6: Ultimate Growth

There were times I thought I would never learn from the adversity I was facing during the initial stages of my diagnosis, and even when I was learning to row and cycle. There were times when I questioned, 'Why me?' But by remaining positive in the long run, I have realised 'Why not me?' Things happen for a reason. I have been able to get through this adversity, learn from it and help others.

I've had my fair share of negative thoughts, and am very aware of them when I do have them, but I try to replace them with more positive thoughts. This isn't easy to do and it takes time to train your brain to do this. It's a continual learning process. When trying things for the first time, I try to think of positive outcomes. Although there are always doubts it's important to push through them. Eventually, if you keep doing this, you will transform the way you think, but it is a constant pursuit.

> 'You cannot tailor-make the situations in life, but you can tailor-make the attitudes to fit those situations.'
> **– Zig Ziglar**

If you believe that you are going to fail, you will; if you believe that you can attain your goal you will take steps to learn to do that.

People have asked me if I have ever received any bad advice while on a journey of learning. Well, opinions vary and I tend to take people's advice and then try to make sense of it myself. What may work for one person may not work for another. There are times when I try to look at my problems as someone else's and detach from them. Then I ask myself,

'What advice would I give to someone experiencing the same problem?' and 'Whose advice would I take?' It is important to try to take a step back and look at a problem from someone else's perspective.

You can take all the advice in the world from others, but it is up to you, the individual, to decide what is best for you. You will understand what choice is right by reviewing the knowledge you have attained up to this point. Through positive thinking and knowledge gained, you will find an alternative path towards any goal or dream.

At times, I have encountered obstacles, such as steep enrolment costs for a course that may help me, but there are always ways around these. There is a wealth of information at our fingertips through the internet, books and mentors. Not everything is based around cost, but I had to look at prioritising the value of the investments I made. If I felt something was vitally important, I would find a way to pay for it. I could sell something I no longer needed, or enquire about payment plans. It is amazing how many times you can actually find the money if you really need to.

Each day, one of the treasures in life that you can have is to seek out knowledge. One of the ways I have done this is to look at a moment in my life where I've had adversity. We all face adversity at some point and we usually come through the other side. What is important to ask is, 'What was the golden lesson from this adversity?' My biggest adversity was probably my diagnosis and, to me, the golden lesson there was that life goes on. I also learnt that I must have all the facts before making any huge decisions that could affect the rest of my life. Don't make hasty decisions with little or

Chapter 6: Ultimate Growth

no information. Be well-informed and knowledgeable, then take it from there.

Another thing I do when looking for information is to sit and make a list of the top-three mentors that I feel may have impartible information. These mentors are usually people I already know, people who have been through similar problems. With these mentors, I have a great wealth of knowledge at my disposal. Mentors give you the opportunity to connect and collaborate with like-minded people so that you can figure out how to attain or take small steps towards your goal. A mentor will help you maximise your potential, help you improve your knowledge and develop your skills. Ask them questions, soak up the answers and, if they can't help, find another mentor who may have the answers. This will still put you one step closer to understanding what you have to do. Open your mind to possibilities you never thought existed and look past the problem with a positive outlook. If you have no mentors, seek one out; there are always people out there who have gone before you. Don't try to reinvent the wheel.

My mentors have come from the worlds I am presently in, such as the cycling community. Although I may ride a trike, which is completely different from riding on two wheels, the racing is the same and, to me, it was important to learn from those who have been doing it for a while. Learning others' tactics, or how they prepare the night before a race, was useful.

For me, it is important to think about what skills I want to add all-year round. Depending on the skill set, it is important to seek out potential learning avenues. This isn't just within my sporting life, but in my daily life as well. I may be great at some things, but there is always room for improvement or for additional skills. Using the skills I already have gives me greater scope to learn.

The difficulties in our lives should be looked at as challenges, stepping stones, chances to gain knowledge. By seeking ultimate growth, you will boost your confidence and your expectations of success, allowing you to realise that you can attain your goals and dreams.

Top: Carol as a young gymnast.
Bottom left: Carol and her father at her graduation as a police constable.
Bottom right: Carol and Russ at their wedding in 1995.

Top: Carol the swimmer.
Bottom: Carol rowing in Italy in 2009.
Inset: Carol starting the 12th Annual Mega Swim.

Top: Finish line of the World Cup in Canada 2013. (Photo courtesy of Tom Skulander.)

Top: Carol on the World Champion podium 2014.

Chapter 7:
Winning Mindset

I will... I will... I will... I will... I will... I'VE DONE IT!!!
I know I can... I know I can... I know I can...
I think I can... I think I can... I think I can...
I know I can... I know I can... I will... I will... I will...

Our behaviour, mindsets and attitudes are the most important tools to reach our full capacity, potential and goals. If you don't believe you can reach your goals, you never will.

I believe that in order to actually have that winning mindset, you have to set your goals and know exactly what you are aiming for. The better you understand your goals, the better the positive mindset you will create.

It is important to ask yourself three questions:
- Do you know what it is you specifically want to achieve?

- Have you implemented stepping stones towards that goal?

- Do you believe you can achieve it?

To tackle the first two questions, there is a goal-setting system called the SMART system.[2]

Be specific in defining your goal. Ask what you want to accomplish and why? Who will help you or be involved?

---

2 SMART criteria are commonly attributed to Peter Drucker's management by objective concept, 1954.

Where do you want to do this and what could possibly hold you back? The more specific your answers are, the easier it will be to put steps in place to be successful.

Make sure that your goals are measurable, as this will allow you to know if you are making progress towards them. If it isn't measurable, you will never know if you are on the right path. Being able to measure your progress will help you stay on track and give you a sense of achievement as you reach each milestone.

Your goal should also be achievable; ask can your goal be accomplished and, if so, how? When your goal is important to you, you will figure out ways to reach it. Is this goal appropriate, or should you be setting your sights higher or lower? Understanding if your goal is achievable will help you develop the right attitude to reach it.

Is your goal realistic? Is it reasonable to believe that you can reach your goal? These questions will help you to understand any hurdles that you may face towards achieving your goal.

Make sure your goal is timely. In other words, put a timeframe around your attainment of this goal. This could be in the form of smaller goals or stepping stones towards the final outcome. Putting timeframes around what you want to accomplish makes your goal real. It could be in the form of smaller daily, weekly, monthly or yearly goals. It is important to set these goals so that you stay focused on achieving the ultimate outcome.

The third question focuses on your mind. Positive thinking can be a powerful tool with which to attain your goals. With

Chapter 7: Winning Mindset

a positive mindset, you are more likely to see possibilities and options. Having this positive mindset will build your motivation, confidence and wellbeing. If you are positive in the belief that you can achieve your goal, you will start to set your goals higher.

A winning mindset will give you a greater involvement in the project. If you are positive about being able to reach your goal and have self-belief you will want to do everything in your power to attain your goal. But being positive isn't always easy; negative influences will always invade our thinking. If your thoughts are negative, you will be more pessimistic and it will be highly likely that you will fail in attaining your goal. So it is important to learn how to be positive and make it a way of life. This can be difficult, but it is important to consciously think about pushing negative thoughts from your head. Be very aware of a negative thought and try to push it from your mind with a positive spin. It is something that you will have to work on. It will take some time, but eventually your mind will instinctually think positively.

Constantly thinking of positive results will help shape who you are and improve your relationships with others. This can only be beneficial in that it will help make you feel inspired and help you when you hit a hurdle.

A winning mindset helps you see your opponent as an ally and not a foe. If you believe in yourself, and your abilities, you will not fear your opponent, but use them to drive you even further than you thought possible. Know your enemy; understand what makes your opponent tick. On days when I don't feel like training, I think about what my competitors are doing, which spurs me to be positive about training. Don't fear your opponent; use them as a positive motivator. A winning mindset is about focusing on success and living up to your potential. Talent alone will not create success; you need to add not only effort, but belief. Use your opponent as a catalyst to push yourself further.

Being positive about what you want to accomplish will assist you in reaching those goals. When you realise that you are able to do this, you will be more encouraged to pursue even bigger goals. If you don't believe in yourself and your abilities, no one else will.

> 'If you really want to touch the sky, don't live downstairs.'
> **– Constance Chuks Friday**

In late 2011, after taking part in my first ever Nationals, I was fast-tracked onto the Australian Para-cycling team. I really knew nothing about racing and was hoping that I could learn from other members of the team. What I didn't count on was a bit of negativity. I have tried to eliminate most of the people from my life who have negative worldviews. We all have those types of friends who can't find anything good in their day. When I encountered negativity within some of the other riders, I was surprised. I was learning a lot about the Para-cycling world and the rules that you have to follow, especially around the Paralympics.

It was a steep learning curve and what I didn't realise was that in 2012 the trike category, which I ride in, was going to be mixed racing in London. By this I mean that men and women in categories T1 and T2 would all be racing together

Chapter 7: Winning Mindset

for one set of medals. In the time trial, there would be a handicap system put in place, but the road race would be a straight-out race: no handicapping, but straight, raw time with all competitors. It became clear that the only race that any woman or T1 man could possibly medal in was the time trial, with handicaps in place.

This information was conveyed to me by another rider, who basically said I had no chance of making the team. The team would be made up of riders whom the selectors felt had medal potential and, because I had never had to race men, I was untested. Well, telling me something negative is like waving a red flag at a bull! I hate negativity, so had to remove myself from listening to this rider and work out what I needed to do in order to make this a positive learning experience. First, I had to arm myself with all the information that I needed from the people who had the answers. For instance, I had to find out what the handicap percentages were, what stepping stones I needed to target and what was the likelihood of making the team. With the knowledge in place, I was able to sit down and, using the SMART system, put everything into perspective. It certainly wasn't the first time I had dealt with negativity in sport. I knew what I was capable of, even if others didn't believe it. I'd been through this with rowing.

As 2012 approached, I looked at the results of the male competitors from 2011 and worked out what I would have to accomplish in order to compete against them. This set me target strength and speed goals, which I could measure over the coming months – not just on the road, but in the lab as well. In June of 2012, the team headed to the World Cup in Segovia, Spain. This was where the head coach and I saw the results from the time trial: what the men had done and what I had done.

Not only had I, on raw time, placed third overall, but I would have won with the handicap put in place, so London was looking good. After the World Cup we were able to ride the actual course used for the time trial and road race events. This gave us a feel for the course and was a fabulous opportunity. I hadn't expected the course to be so hard.

We were scheduled to race at Brands Hatch, which is a car race circuit. Part of the course was on the circuit and the rest was on roads outside the track. The course would be tough for hand-cyclists and trikes because of the tight corners and big climbs. The Australian team was lucky to have sports scientists with us. They were able to get all the course data, which was then translated into a computer program that we could use in the lab on a velotron.[3] This enabled me to ride the course over and over until I knew it inside and out. I knew I had to feel the fear of this course and get comfortable being uncomfortable. Some of the hills were certainly going to test me. This preparation proved I had a great chance of winning on this course.

When I returned to Melbourne for the last-ditch training, I put everything I had into my preparation. This wasn't just the physical side, but also the mental side. Even though the course was difficult, I had to get my mind believing that it was made just for my strengths. I did a fair bit of imagery

---

[3] The velotron is a bike attached to a computer screen, which allows the course to be put in front of the rider with all gradients included.

Chapter 7: Winning Mindset

work; I saw myself riding, knew what I would do on each part of the course, how fast I would take each corner and climb. I wanted this information implanted in my mind by the time I arrived at the course on race day. There were no surprises or fear; I knew what I had to do.

When the start list came out for the time trial, I decided to use my opponents to the best of my ability. I saw I was starting sixth last on the list, with David Stone from Great Britain starting one minute behind me and my main female competitor, Marie-Eve Croteau, listed to start second last and Hans-Peter Durst the reigning male World Champion to start last.

At that time, I had no idea that Marie-Eve wasn't starting and I decided to use the fact that David Stone was only a minute behind me as motivation. I had done my homework; I knew how fast David and Hans-Peter could go, so knew I had to stay in front for as long as possible. I worked out where I believed David would pass me on the course, so aimed to make it past that point before he caught me.

Only one lap of the course was required and I was sent on my way. At this point, I could have ridden the course blindfolded. I had done my homework and was ready. At the start of the race, I passed three riders within a very short time and kept thinking about how much I believed in my ability and myself, but also repeated *stay in front of David, stay in front of David* in my head. He didn't catch me at the point I expected him to, which was fantastic and spurred me on. But then, out of nowhere, he caught me, not that far from the finish. I had two hills to conquer and could not let him get too far away from me.

The noise down the finishing straight was incredible, with people cheering and pounding on the side boards. You could feel the noise. That's the only way to describe it. Then, all of a sudden, it was over. I knew I had given it my all as I had nothing left in the tank. I couldn't even peddle to our bay in the sheds. My legs were spent and I was lucky our physiotherapist was there to push me along. Now it was a waiting game. I had no idea what time David had done and there were still other riders to come – including good riders from Italy, America, France and Germany – who could pip me at the post.

Once all the riders were in and I was told that I had won, I spoke with David, who told me he was very surprised he hadn't caught me earlier. Both he and Hans-Peter were extremely courteous and supportive in congratulating me on the win. It was an amazing ride, but if I didn't believe in myself and have the right mindset I don't think I would have done as well.

Believing that you can win or attain whatever goal you are striving for is one thing, but in order to do it you have to take the necessary actions. If I hadn't done the 'homework' – learning what I had to do, training on the course (even if it was on a computer) and periodically testing myself to see if I was on track – then I don't believe I would have been as successful. No detail is beneath you or unimportant, especially when it comes to having a winning mindset, because it's the combination of all those details that brings your dream to life.

I've been a positive person for most of my life. If you aren't a naturally positive person, learning how to have a winning mindset may not happen overnight. If you have never been a positive person it can be very daunting and you may need to look for assistance. This could include the use of a psychologist. Psychologists are a fantastic way to help you on the right track – even Olympians use them.

I remember sitting at the VIS one day listening to a talk given by David Crawshay, one of Australia's best and most-respected rowers. He was talking to us about the use of the sport psychology services available and I was quite surprised to hear that he had used this tool to help boost his winning mindset. He told us he needed the assistance to combat nerves and negative thoughts at the start of races.

I was surprised because he came across as invincible and so self-assured. He had won a gold medal in the men's double sculls with Scott Brennan at the 2008 Beijing Olympics and seemed to me to be the perfect athlete. So it was amazing to hear that he had needed this help. He had used this service to try to wipe out any negative doubts he had about his rowing. The fact that he looked for help to overcome this just proved how perfect an athlete he was. He didn't want anything to stand in his way of attaining his goals.

I was lucky to have been taught mindset-influencing strategies as a young swimmer, such as visualisation and positive self-talk. Strategies like these can help you deal with the pressure of competition, enhance your performance and teach you relaxation techniques, which help create winning mindsets. I have learned, though, that different things work for different people. You have to work out what is best for you to help you create a positive mindset.

It is important to pay attention to your mind and try to stop those negative thoughts from inhabiting your brain. Positive thoughts will help you see the positive side of setbacks and make you more confident, creative and resourceful. This will enable you to overcome them. Negative thoughts make you unproductive, pessimistic and uninspired, and will stop you in your tracks before you realise your goals.

There will be times you feel you can't go on, or that no approach seems to work. These are the times when you must focus on the result. You have to find the passion that you had when you set your goal and see how you can get help to proceed. It is critical to understand why you can't progress and it is equally important to get feedback and get into a positive mindset. You have to focus on what you, as an individual, can control.

If you really want to teach yourself positive thinking, there are a number of things that can help. These can be done on a daily basis:

- Each night, write at least one positive statement about what you are trying to achieve. This will help with training your mind in positive self-talk. It will take time to learn how to be extremely positive, but this will give you confidence to move forward.

- Don't look at the 'big picture' too often. Sometimes you can get lost in the final destination and neglect to think about all those baby steps on the journey. It is important to be good at the 'one percent' things. All those 'one percentages' add up, making your efforts more efficient and effective. Focus on those little things and they will eventually lead you to your final destination. The focus should be on the journey, not the destination.

- Come up with a 'belief' motto and say it each day when you wake up. You may not believe it at the start, but by saying it every day your brain will eventually start to believe it. It can be something as simple as 'I can do it!' One of mine is 'Dare to face your fears! Believe in yourself and you can accomplish anything!' By mastering the power of positive thinking, you will well and truly be on your way towards positively dealing with obstacles.

Chapter 8:
Guaranteed Results

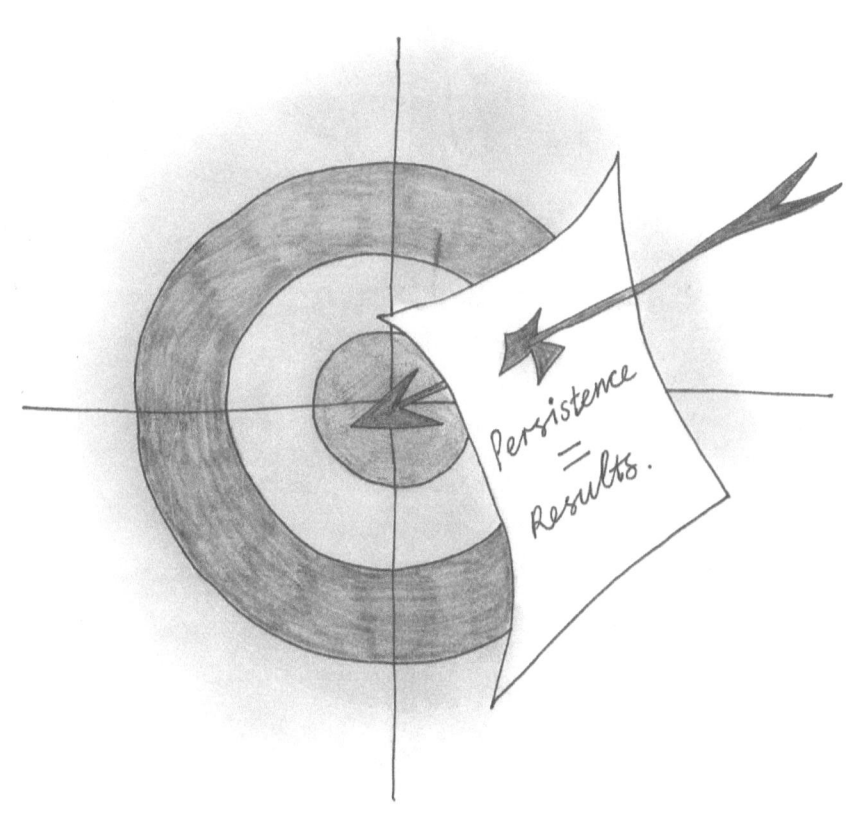

We've all seen those advertisements for fitness or weight loss products with *Guaranteed Results* emblazoned on them. Well, I'm here to tell you that they *can* be guaranteed – but only if you are persistent. This chapter is all about persistence. It's very easy to give up if things aren't going your way, but with persistence comes reward. The temptation to quit will be greatest just before you succeed and see results!

I've always been happy having a lot of structure in my life and tend to plan and set goals for most things I do. Some might say that this makes me obsessive, but I am also open to change and realise that things rarely stay the same. But with those changes come challenges and, in order to get past those challenges, you must have perseverance. If you persevere, the small obstacles you overcome build up over time to become something much bigger and better.

At times, your perseverance can wane, but it is important to remember that the more persistent you are the stronger you get. We all make excuses not to continue with something. Sometimes it's a lack of motivation, obstacles that appear, or plain procrastination when other parts of our life invade.

It is important to work on a few short-term goals that will show you that you can progress to that ultimate goal. This persistence will give you extra focus and produce quality results.

You know what causes your procrastination and have the choice to give up or be the one who persists and continues. If you persist, you will beat the odds, and the more you do something, the better you will become at it.

The more you persist, the greater your sense of purpose. As you reach each small goal, you will realise that your persistence has paid off. If you want guaranteed results, do absolutely nothing: you successfully get nowhere.

> 'The habit of persistence is the habit of victory.'
> **– Herbert Kaufman (American writer)**

If you persevere, you will eventually be victorious; if you don't persevere, you won't attain the results you are looking for.

In 2007, after I was told by a Rowing Australia staff member that I would never be good or fit enough to make a national team, I decided not to give in to his negativity and persevere. By making the team in 2008, I proved to myself that, by devising a strategy and following it to the last letter, anything could be possible.

In January of 2008, and with the Australian National Rowing Championships getting closer, I put a huge amount of work into my training. I got better at rowing in a single, as this was going to decide who would be seat racing to make the LTA4+. An Australian LTA4+ boat was going to the first World Cup in May that year in Munich, Germany to attempt to qualify for Beijing. I really had no idea which other women would attempt to get a seat.

Chapter 8: Guaranteed Results

The LTA4+ is the Paralympic class that I was classified for. In this class, rowers are in a coxed four boat and can use their legs, trunk and arms (LTA), so there are no real modifications to the boat. The coxswain doesn't have a disability, but the rowers can have a wide range of disabilities, such as vision impairment, amputation, MS, Cerebral Palsy – any type of condition that will fit the classification criteria. It is also a mixed-gender boat, with two men and two women. With only two seats for women and no way of knowing how many would be nominated, I was driven to work even harder.

I headed to Sydney for Nationals and for my first-ever singles race at a national level. It turned out there were just three of us racing in the LTA women's single, but one of the girls, Julia, who I was rowing with in the double, was in the ID (intellectual disability) category and wasn't eligible for the LTA4+. This left me and another woman from Canberra, Brandie (vision impaired), as the only two eligible rowers. I didn't win that race – Julia did – but I won the silver from Brandie. There were a number of guys rowing, so the racing was intense; we all wanted to see who would get the chance to seat race. A few of us were invited to the selection trials to see who would be in the boat and find out if we were actually fast enough to go to the World Cup.

It turned out two guys – Pete and Gene, both amputees – were to join Brandie and I in the boat, along with a cox, Lisa, from my own club, who I had talked into nominating. We definitely struggled; Brandie, in particular, who had never rowed from the bow seat, struggled with the timing and, at times, hit me hard in the back with her oar. It almost brought me to tears. But we persevered and finally got our shit together. It certainly didn't happen overnight, but we were at least rowing well enough for the selectors to think we could go to the World Cup and earn a spot for Beijing.

With Paralympic rowing, there are only ever a maximum of twelve boats in each of the events. Nine of these spots must be earned at the World Championships the year before. The last three spots have to be earned at the first World Cup of the Paralympic year. In 2008, two spots would come from the final and the third was a wild card entry. Nowadays, this last spot belongs to the host country. So we knew that we had to place in the top two in order to get to Beijing.

We really didn't have much training leading up – just a couple of camps for a few days at a time – so we as a crew decided we would organise our own training week. Everyone came to Melbourne and I set up a week of training out of my rowing club: the Yarra Yarra Rowing Club. We did this out of our own desire to do the best we could, with Pete coming down from Queensland, Gene from New South Wales and Brandie from Canberra. Together we persevered with a week of training. Brandie was injured, so we had a fill in for her, but at least the other four of us – Lisa, Gene, Pete and I – were able to get some great time together. I don't believe we ever thought we could fail. I had made no plans for after the World Cup, except to train for Beijing, which would be in the August of the same year. Since we had a good possibility of going, we were outfitted and sized for the team gear. In my head, there was no such thing as failure. I didn't even give it a thought; we were going.

The time arrived to head to a staging camp at the Sydney International Regatta Centre (SIRC) before heading to Munich. I must say, we had some pretty good rows. The

Chapter 8: Guaranteed Results

coaches and selectors were happy with the progress that we had made and it was looking very positive. We headed overseas with the rest of the Australian Rowing Team. It was an amazing experience to be wearing the gold and green of Australia, and to be included with the able-bodied team. Rowing is one of few all-inclusive international sports, with Para-rowing included alongside the able-bodied World Championships. This was my first-ever national team and, boy, it felt good. I was so happy to have ignored that initial email from the Rowing Australia staff member. All it took was the right mindset and a bit of perseverance to get where I was at that moment.

We settled in not far from the rowing course and spent the next couple of days setting up the boat and doing a bit of training on the course. There were only a handful of other countries taking part in the LTA4+ category, as most had already qualified the year before. We were up against China, South Africa, Denmark and Japan, so there was going to be a heat, but only a race for lanes. The fastest in the heat would get the best lane for the final. We certainly didn't have a good row in the heat, as some of our oars missed water at the start. We definitely weren't going to get the best lane for the final. You could call it inexperience, but I think we were all a bit nervous.

China had blitzed everyone, so it was going to be a race for second place. There was also the wild card entry, but we certainly couldn't pin our hopes on that. We really needed to sit down and regroup, work out what had gone wrong, then forget about how bad the row was, wipe it from our minds, and focus on the final. We knew that we kept losing ground in the third 250 metres. The Para-rowing crews race over 1,000 metres, while able-bodied rowers race over 2,000. It was important to make sure we built the race and really pushed on the third 250.

The day of the final arrived. It was ridiculous how nervous I was. As we got to the course, all I wanted to do was throw up, but I certainly didn't let on to any of my crewmates. Gene was the only one of us who had any international experience and, as we got in the boat and made our way to the start, he turned and took my hand and said, 'Let's do this.'

All of a sudden, my nerves disappeared and I was ready to race. Mind you, the weather wasn't the best and I give a pat on the back to Lisa, our cox, who, at 17, did an amazing job keeping us straight at the start. The water was choppy and the wind was massive, but, as the lights went green and the beeper sounded, off we went. We had a great start and Lisa kept us building through each 250-metre stretch. China had once again taken off and the only way they weren't going to qualify was if they had a mechanical issue, so the race was on for second.

As we approached the third 250, Lisa called for a push and, for the first time ever, I felt the boat surge and, in my peripheral vision, I saw the other boats beside us. But we needed to hold it over the last 250 metres, which I believed we had. But when we crossed the finish line, it was a blanket finish with Denmark, South Africa and us. None of the crews knew who had crossed in second place; it even went to a photo finish. In the end, Denmark took second, South Africa took third and we were fourth, with only 0.8 seconds between second and fourth place. I was gutted, as I am sure my crewmates were.

Chapter 8: Guaranteed Results

We had given it our all, done exactly what was asked of us, but failed to qualify. Our last hope was the wild card, but that was eventually given to South Africa, who didn't have any other boats qualified. Australia had already qualified in two other classes.

As we pulled into the dock, I realised I wasn't even going to be able to get out of the boat; my legs were gone. I was lifted out and asked if I wanted a wheelchair. I told them no. I just wanted to lie on the dock and, with my sunglasses on, I cried like a baby. (Thank God for sunnies.) My dream of representing my country on the biggest world stage after all those years was gone. I didn't even know what I was going to do when I got home because I really believed that we would all be heading to Beijing!

Later, we sat down with the High Performance Director of RA and our coach and were told that our race was one of the best of the World Cup, and that Para-Rowing had come of age. We had executed our race plan perfectly and done our best. That was all anyone could ask for. That certainly helped, but the disappointment of not qualifying would stay with us for awhile. I didn't think that, at 47, I would be able to continue training the way I had been so, at that low point, I figured my dream was gone forever.

That is until I got a swift kick up the backside via cyberspace by my sister, who reminded me that it wasn't about the destination but that it was about the journey and that my journey didn't have to end here. She said to take it a minute, a day, a week, a month and a year at a time. Just keep persevering until you aren't enjoying it any more. She was right. What did my age have to do with it? If I was enjoying it, and still going fast enough to make the crew, I should keep going. She also sent me a small credit card-sized card that said *Behind every success is effort ... Behind every effort is passion ... Behind every passion is someone with the courage to try.*

So continue I did, making the crew again in 2009 for the World Championships. It was a slightly different crew. Pete and I were there, and Lisa was still coxing; the two new rowers were Henry and Alex. We had some challenges, as Henry had never rowed sweep and was vision-impaired, so needed to sit in the stroke seat. But we overcame our difficulties and made it into the final, which no one expected. We didn't exactly have the best row in the final finishing sixth, but we believed that we had finally arrived. After all, we had made it to the final and would be able to look towards London and the 2012 Paralympics.

We all really looked forward to the World Championships in 2010, as they were going to be held in New Zealand. Again, there were some slight changes to the crew, with a new cox and man, but we thought we would be able to pull it together. We were invited to the selection trials and then, a week before the trials, we were uninvited via a teleconference. This shocked all of us and the reasons given were ridiculous – all of which I challenged.

To me and the rest of the crew, this was like dangling a carrot in front of us for the past two years, then yanking it away. We truly believed that it was because they weren't interested in our category and had come up with trivial reasons not to include us. I continued to challenge what we had been told and even approached the athlete's advocate, who also got no response from the then High Performance Director. But I

Chapter 8: Guaranteed Results

continued to row, believing that they would have to change their minds eventually and when, in early 2011, they still hadn't, I had to make some decisions about what I wanted to do. Should I give up on my goal of the Paralympics and just row as a Masters Rower or try another sport?

Alex, who I had been in the crew with in 2009, had started cycling at the end of 2010. She called me and told me they had a trike category in Para-cycling. As I said earlier, I believe nothing ever stays the same and, with perseverance, and by looking for another way around a problem, you can achieve anything. I still had that goal of representing my country and, if it wasn't going to be in rowing, I decided it would be cycling. I would at least give it my best try. I certainly came across so many negative people within the elite rowing community, but I always believed there was never a set time by which to reach a goal; I would continue as long as it was important and enjoyable to me.

When I look back at pictures from those rowing years, I tend to shudder because, even though I was doing well in the sport, I don't look very fit. So, in 2011, I made the decision to get fitter and stronger. I had been given a challenge by the Cycling Australia Para-cycling coaching staff: if I did this, they would build me a new trike. Considering I was riding a 22kg steel-framed trike, while the rest of the world was on 14kg trikes, I made sure that this was one challenge I wasn't going to fail.

There is certainly no easy way to lose weight, but I persevered for months with no sugar and no alcohol, I also watched every morsel I put in my mouth and, within six months, I had lost about 12 kgs. I used the same strategies I have used through all the sports I have been involved with. I made an action plan, kept a log of what I was eating and what my energy output was. It worked. Cycling Australia held true to their word and presented me with a new trike in March 2012 at a camp in Canberra. This proved that rewards come if you follow through with your action plans.

Even at the beginning, I always wrote down my goals, whether it be a specific time that I wanted to achieve while swimming, or a time over 1,000 metres for rowing, or an average time trial cycling speed. It is important to write your goals down and post them somewhere where you will see them multiple times a day. I also think it is important to tell someone you trust about your goal, someone who can be a confidant, coach, or really anyone who'll show support. The more you see and hear about your goal, the more real it will become.

I also sit down every year with my coach to write an action plan. Having this plan, with smaller goals along the way, will help you persist throughout the year. Knowing the steps you have to take makes it easier to continue on the right path.

With persistence, the biggest obstacles will fall and even the most ambitious achievements become within reach. I know that I can achieve whatever I choose to achieve and the process begins with the decision and commitment to do it. No achievement is ever easy and you owe it – not just to yourself, but to the people who believe in you – to transform that goal-reaching possibility into reality. The dreams you have are in your hands and are yours for the taking. All it will take is a little persistence.

Chapter 9:
Beyond Limits

Our lives are not determined by what happens to us, but by how we react to what happens to us. An MS diagnosis was not going to define who I was. I had choices regarding how I was going to live my life. I wanted to live beyond the perceived limits MS would place on me. The first doctor that diagnosed me said that I would never do sport again and I was not going to let someone dictate what I could or couldn't do. It was up to me to push those boundaries and see how I could incorporate living with MS with sport. It would mean going beyond those boundaries that were perceived by that first doctor, but, really, it's about the power of the mind and what it can accomplish.

This chapter is about pushing yourself beyond your comfort zone and grabbing new opportunities that you might otherwise miss. Push yourself beyond what you or anyone else thinks you are capable of and believe.

Here's why pushing yourself beyond your limits is important:
- It helps you learn and acquire new skill sets. These skill sets can relate to different areas of your life. They could be people skills, social skills, life skills or any skills relating to a specific task, which are known as hard skills. Pushing beyond our perceived capabilities helps us learn. It gives us valuable experience, which is needed to overcome obstacles in our path.

- Pushing beyond your limits helps improve your self-worth. It will help you understand that you can get through tough situations. It will also give you the ability and strength to try new things and to realise that failure is only a stepping stone towards success.

- It will force you to explore new opportunities and challenges. If you don't push beyond your limits, you will always stay within your comfort zone and never improve or learn new things. The key differences between a boring, unsatisfying life and one of excitement, success and growth is how willing you are to escape your comfort zone.

- Pushing past your comfort zone helps with success. Remember, failure is just a stepping stone to success. You will find out what works and what doesn't. As Steve Bloom says: 'The only thing stopping you from reaching your goals and dreams are your limits'.

- Going beyond your perceived limits can open new doors for you and help you become mentally stronger. Unfortunately, most of us have limiting beliefs which influence our performance. By pushing beyond those limits, we can influence our choices and actions, enabling us to grow and evolve. Adopting a mindset that says we can surpass the limits we've set for ourselves will help us improve.

There are several ways to push beyond our limits. One can be by training harder than we ever have in order to attain a goal. Another could be to attempt something new, pushing our beliefs beyond where we think they can go.

I believe I have been blessed with the power to push beyond my limits, but, in saying that, I was taught from an early age about pushing my limits in training. It came through coaches that I had when I was a swimmer and, as I have grown, and changed sports and coaches, I have learnt that no matter how bad a training session or race hurts, I will always have that little bit more to give at the end. I'm not scared of the pain associated with pushing myself and, in fact, that feeling is addictive. Having a good coach to assist you with pushing through your limits can counteract any negative thoughts you might have. Having someone tell you that you *can* do it will help get those positive thoughts running through your brain.

Going beyond your limits is all about playing mind games with yourself. It's about tricking your mind into believing that the training you are doing isn't hurting, and about tricking your mind into believing you are giving less than a hundred percent effort. Most of us have bucket lists, and I am no exception. One of my bucket list items is the Seven Peaks challenge in Victoria. The challenge involves climbing the Seven Peaks: Mt. Baw Baw, Mt. Buffalo, Mt. Buller, Dinner Plains, Falls Creek, Mt. Hotham, and Lake Mountain. I don't think I would attempt to climb them in the time allotted for the official challenge; I would just like to climb them on my trike. There are incredible climbs out there that are extremely steep. One day, I would love to say that I climbed them all.

In 2013, while away with my cycling club, I did one of the

climbs – Mt. Buffalo – and, at the time, it was a real mind game to get up that mountain, which was 23 kms straight up with an average 5% gradient and a maximum of 11%. The good thing about trike riding is you can go as slow as you want and will not fall over because of the three wheels. The toughest part of the climb was coming down. I wasn't that great at cornering back then, so it was definitely scarier than going up.

In 2014, while up in Bright once again on our cycling club women's weekend, I decided I would try to climb Mt. Hotham on the Saturday and then tackle Mt. Buffalo again on the Sunday. Saturday morning dawned beautiful and it was time to tackle that bucket list item: Mt. Hotham. I knew that this was going to be a tough ask because my trike weighs 14 kgs and the climb to the village of Hotham is 32.4 kms, with a peak of 1,347 metres, an average gradient of 4% and a maximum gradient of 18%. I didn't know if I would be able to do it.

But it is amazing what you can accomplish when you have a great group of people around you and you try to push beyond your own perceived limits. I had left earlier than the rest of the group, but I also realised what my limits were; instead of riding from Bright to Harrietville, which is located at the base of Mt. Hotham and is an extra 40-km return, I decided to drive there. I figured that a 100-km ride (with 32 of those uphill) was a bit beyond what I really wanted to do. I knew that by giving myself a head start, the group would eventually catch me on the climb, so it was a goal to try to see how much of the climb I could do before they all passed me.

Chapter 9: Beyond Limits

One of the ways I am able to push beyond my limits is to break my goals down into smaller parts. I was told that the climb up Mt. Hotham could be broken into three parts, each about 10 kms. The first 10 kms were difficult and involved steady climbing. The second 10 kms undulated and the last third of the mountain had enormous climbs; big, fast downhills; and a killer last 2 kms! That 18% I was talking about! But then it rewards you with a 1 km downhill into the village.

From Harrietville, I warmed up by riding up and down the main road, then started the climb. In hindsight, I would have liked a longer warm-up because everyone was right: the first 10 kms were tough! It made me question right from the start whether I would be able to make it up. It was fantastic to be out riding with like-minded people because I received so much support from every rider going up. I didn't know most of the people riding by me, but was spurred on by their encouragement.

I don't think my legs have ever burned so much. My muscles screamed with every pedal stroke. Some people would say I was nuts to continue, but when you have a goal you do what you must to reach it. Fortunately, the middle 10 kms were lovely, which took my mind to a positive place and gave my legs a much-needed reprieve. By the time I started the last 10 kms my legs felt better and my resolve had strengthened. I was going to make it to the top.

Then I hit the last 2 kms ... Oh my God! This climb was the hardest thing I have ever done in my life to this point. I really had to play some head games with myself. The first thing I did was not look up to see how far I had to go, nor look at my Garmin computer for the same reason. I kept my eyes on the ground in front of me and the beautiful scenery to the left of me. I had to keep my legs moving, no matter how slowly I went. When I finally saw the tunnel to the village with the Hotham sign on the other side of it, I let off a silent *Hooray!* in my head. I think if I had a finish line and wasn't so tired I would have thrown my hands in the air, like I had just won the Tour de France!

I made my way to the General Store to validate that I had made it to the top with a stamp in my Seven Peaks Passport. I had attained my bucket list item and couldn't have been happier. I was so excited that I had actually made it that I forgot that there would be some climbing on the way back down the mountain! To me, it didn't make sense: I am going *down* a mountain, but have to climb *up* it to get there! The rest of the downhill certainly made up for those climbs. In the end, it took me two hours and fifty-six minutes to climb from Harrietville and an hour and ten to come down.

But my weekend challenge wasn't over, as I wanted to climb Mt. Buffalo the following day. So, after a quick splash in the river in the centre of Bright, an amazing meal with the rest of the women and a good night's sleep, I was ready to tackle the next mountain on the Sunday morning. I once again headed out earlier than everyone else and started the climb up Mt. Buffalo. I knew that I could get to the top of this mountain because I had done it last year, but my legs were feeling the effects from the day before. I had to keep turning my legs over. Again, I had a number of riders pass me and spur me on and even some riders on the way back down shaking their heads in disbelief, with one even raising his arm in the air, saying 'I don't believe you!' I just smiled and

Chapter 9: Beyond Limits

said 'Good morning'. Not many of those riders would have ever seen a trike, let alone see one climbing a mountain! These little proud moments make me happy I push myself beyond where people think I can go.

Without pushing myself, I would have never made it to the London Paralympics. After our crew was dumped by Rowing Australia in 2010, I continued to believe that someone would come to the rescue and reinstate the crew, so continued to train as if things would be okay right into 2011. But I finally realised that if I did want to be in London I would have to re-evaluate what I was doing and maybe try something else. So this is where cycling came into the picture. Obviously when I did my first race, which was the 2011 Australian National Para-Cycling Championships in Queensland, I wasn't even thinking about London. I had never done a cycle race, so just wanted to see how I would go. Pushing beyond my perceived limits gave me the opportunity to explore new challenges and options, which I will never regret doing!

There will always be people who are negative towards you trying to push beyond what they might believe you are capable of, but it is important to disregard what they say and not let their negativity enter your brain. There will be times when you won't believe that you can push those barriers. It is important, during those times, that you don't let it continue for too long. If you feel that you are pushing beyond your limits and are only partially attaining your goal it may be time to re-evaluate what you are trying to achieve and try a different tactic.

You may start assuming you will never get beyond the limits

that you have set for yourself, so this is when you have to take a step back and look at the situation with a different perspective. This is where a good coach, mentor or like-minded person will come in handy, so use them for their perspectives. Be in the moment with them, just like when I was climbing those mountains. All those people – some I knew, some I didn't – gave me encouragement. They helped me push through my limits, and these sorts of people will help you as well.

There are ways of learning how to push yourself by doing little things. A lot of us just take each day as it comes without doing something new and different. One way of pushing your limits, which isn't necessarily exercise-related, is to try to speak to at least one new person a day. It could be in the street, in your office building, on public transport, or standing in a queue – literally anywhere. Most of us don't say hello to strangers because we are so consumed with our own thoughts that we don't notice anyone else. Remember to look up and be in the moment. Look people in the eye and just say 'g'day' or 'good morning', as those few little words could lead to amazing things. You never know who you will meet. You may be nervous, but this will push your limits, so just smile and think of how surprised they will be when you say hello. It will give you both a sense of community.

Another way of pushing your limits is to take on a new challenge. When speaking to groups, no matter what age they are, I always pose a question: 'What would you attempt to do if you knew you couldn't fail?' At times, we become so scared of what other people will think of us that we don't try new things. We worry we will look silly or that we won't be any good. But how many people are really looking at us

Chapter 9: Beyond Limits

when we take on a new challenge? Most of the time, this is all in our heads, so it is important to get past this, push past the limits we place on ourselves and just do it. We sometimes get too comfortable in our daily lives that we don't think we need to get out of that comfort zone, but if you don't you will be standing still your whole life. By pushing those limits, you challenge yourself to be a better you.

One last way of pushing your limits is by using imagery. Many athletes will use this type of training. There are two types of imagery: internal and external perspective. Internal involves seeing yourself doing whatever it is you are pushing your limits to accomplish; external is like watching a video of yourself that someone has taken. Imagery can help you in a number of ways. It can increase your confidence by presenting a perfect outcome. It can also help calm you if you are nervous and assist with actual skills: you can improve technique by visualising doing something.

I was taught to use imagery when I first started swimming. It was useful when preparing for a race. I would sit in a dark room picturing not just my race, but my approach to the marshalling area, stepping behind the starting blocks and starting. I'd then see each and every stroke I took until I finished and touched the wall. When I got good at this imagery, I would use a stopwatch, as if I was timing myself swimming. Eventually, I got so good at it that I would stop the watch at my desired time. This actually translated into the pool and I was able to push through difficult time barriers. Imagery is a very valuable tool, no matter what your goal is.

The way you visualise attaining your goal affects how the

process will inevitably unfold. Seeing and expecting success will play a key role in the outcome. Are you willing to escape your comfort zone, that place where you are content to be? If you can push beyond the contentment and strive for something more you will eventually feel the excitement and success of growth. This will ultimately take you to a completely new dimension, one you didn't know existed.

Most high achievers I know are constantly testing themselves. Personally, I do this to see what I can ultimately achieve. It shows me what does and doesn't work. Push through your comfort zone. Sometimes you may fail, but you will ultimately use those failures to achieve great success. I will never put any limits on my possible achievements because I have found that anything is possible.

Chapter 10:
Discovering Gold

Nothing ever happens in life exactly as we picture it, so it is important to look at the lessons we have learnt along the way. *Discovering Gold* is about looking at the past lessons you have learnt and using them to improve and discover your own 'Pot of Gold'.

But why are past lessons and mistakes important to us?

It is important we constantly move forward in our lives. However, sometimes we become stuck and don't know how to reach those goals. By looking back at times when we felt the same way, we can use lessons that have been imparted on us in the past to learn, improve and move forward. You can think back and realise that you have learned valuable lessons. What worked and what didn't? Will those same lessons apply to the problem you're facing now? Will they translate to this situation? Did outside influences help or harm your attempts to attain your goal? Looking back at the past is a self-study, which will help ensure you don't repeat the same mistakes and will hopefully give you insight on how to move forward.

It is important to assess your goals and make sure they are important to you. Is there anything that you want to change or improve? Ask yourself if there are times in your past when you have tried to reach the same goal and failed. Why did you fail? It's a good idea to write down what you did wrong so you can change it for the future. Once it is on paper, it becomes real.

Learning from our mistakes can be the most important lessons we ever learn. Time can be an excellent teacher. If we learn from our mistakes, we can stop ourselves from making the same ones repeatedly. It will help you learn to make good decisions and choices. If you refuse to learn from your mistakes, you will continue to fail, have bad experiences and make wrong decisions. Learning from those mistakes, instead of projecting blame, will present you with a valuable lesson. You can even learn from other people's mistakes. If you don't learn, you will make the same mistakes continuously; your results will never change until you are forced to learn. Learning from our mistakes enables us to progress towards our goals. It gives us greater insight, which helps us understand how to reach our goals.

Failure is the road to success, but many people are scared of it. I believe that without failure you won't have success. It is an inevitable part of the equation in the formula for success. Failure is a positive stepping stone towards achieving your goals. With failure comes knowledge and this is where we learn from past mistakes that have led to failure. It is important to use failure to learn, grow and ultimately succeed.

The road to *Discovering Gold*, by learning from those lessons, assessing our goals and dealing with failures, makes us more confident in our abilities. If you have the self-confidence to succeed and belief in your abilities, you will succeed. If you have confidence, you can anticipate a successful outcome. Learning from past mistakes and moving forward gives us great confidence.

After my first National Para-Cycling Championships in

Chapter 10: Discovering Gold

2011, the head coach, Peter Day, and a number of others told me I was the fastest T2 woman they had ever seen ride anywhere in the world. I had no real idea of what I was doing during the races; I just went out and gave it my all. In the process, I had won all my races, although I really didn't have much competition. My first World Cup was in Sydney in 2011 and a few riders from around the world attended. There was only one other female, from South Africa. We were racing with the men, who I assumed I would keep up with. I kept up for about 4 kms, then remained with just a couple of the guys. In the end, I was awarded the gold medal, as I was the first female home! I started to believe I was the fastest female in the world and headed into my first World Championships with that in mind. I believed I would win, that was all there was to it. Coming in at any other position wasn't even on my radar.

I headed to Denmark for the 2011 World Para-Cycling Championships with my 22kg steel-framed trike and assumed I would win. Placing second after the time trial was certainly a rude awakening. You see, a French-Canadian woman had been told the same thing, that she was 'the fastest T2 female in the world' – and she was! I was absolutely devastated by the outcome. I didn't know that I hadn't won and was sitting on a wind trainer in our tent, which happened to be right beside the Canadian tent, when I saw the drug testers heading in to see Marie-Eve, the Canadian. I then heard the rest of the team cheering. I knew right then that she had won – and, boy, did that hurt! I came to Denmark thinking there was no way I could lose and here I was, sitting there listening to others cheer for someone else's win! I was devastated, even though I had just come second in the world! I had to regroup and realise that, even though I had only been riding competitively for about five months, and only had a coach for the last two, I was second in the world! Once I had worked this through my brain, I was able to be happy and congratulate myself.

But, looking at this, what did I learn? It was important to sit back and look at not only my performance, but also my way of thinking. I had to dissect my performance, actually breaking the races apart to see where I needed to improve. One of the biggest areas I looked at was the other competitors. What was the difference between them and me? I realised I certainly wasn't as fit as I could be, not when compared to the others. It was important to take this into account and become more serious about my diet and fitness. It didn't hurt that our head coach and his assistant sat me down just before we left Denmark and told me that if I came back fitter and stronger in the New Year, they would build me a new trike. Between the hunger of wanting to win and the offer of a new trike, it was a goal that I was happy to tackle head-on.

I also looked at the race itself to see where I hadn't performed well. It was the climbs and corners; these needed a lot of work! To tackle this, I was going to have to speak with my coach about working on those aspects, then incorporate more technical drills for the cornering and climb more hills within my workouts.

As for my health and fitness, I came home from Denmark and set about completely overhauling my life. I made the decision to really watch my diet, and cut out alcohol and sugar completely. This meant I wouldn't even have a coffee, as I couldn't drink it without – two or three sugars. It was tough, but I had people who supported me along the way. My husband, as the cook, was diligent in his food preparation

Chapter 10: Discovering Gold

and I knew I was motivated enough to continue. A month or so later, I read with great interest an email that was sent to me through a subscription I have to the website of motivational speaker, Craig Harper. It was titled 'Motivation is Not the Answer', so I read on with great interest!

The following lines certainly made me think:

> 'Motivation (on its own) rarely leads to any kind of lasting positive transformation. Commitment, on the other hand, is a non-negotiable mindset. It's absolute. It's a force. Unwavering. Constant. Powerful. Unlike motivation, it's not a day-to-day proposition; it's your default setting. It's not a 'sometimes' emotion but rather, an 'all-the-time' habit. Committed people make things happen, even in the absence of motivation.'

Reading this renewed my determination to become a fitter and stronger rider.

For me, that meant that I had to make sure I was accountable for literally everything that went into my mouth. To do this, I kept a diary. I wrote everything down. No matter how small, it went into the diary. I also measured myself weekly – not just by standing on the scales, but with a tape measure, too. Sometimes we concentrate too much on the weight loss and forget that other factors affect our body measurements. As I took charge of my food intake and increased my training, my clothes felt much looser, even if the weight wasn't dropping as much.

Within three months, I found that my body was certainly

changing. Not only was I losing weight, but my coach and I had really increased the distances I was riding and incorporating more hill climbing. That December, we had a training camp in Bright, Victoria and, on one of the days, I was told to do a three-to-four-hour ride to build my endurance. I decided to ride to the town of Beechworth and back. I didn't think this would be too hard. However, about 10 kms from Beechworth, I hit the biggest bloody hill I had ever tackled. It took me almost forty minutes to ride 5 kms due to the 12–14% gradient of the hill. Several times, I thought *this is nuts* and wanted to turn around. But then that word 'commitment' kept popping into my head, so I just kept going. It turned out to be the longest, toughest ride I had done until that point, but it proved to me that I could do this type of training. If I wanted to be number one in the world, I was going to have to keep doing it.

That same month, I went to watch the Australian Para Track Cycling Championships in Melbourne and saw our head coach there. I think he was stunned when he realised it was me speaking to him, as I had really taken what he had said to the limit! I had lost a few kilos at that point and was certainly looking fitter than when he had last seen me.

In March 2012, we had a Para-cycling camp at the AIS in Canberra and, true to his word, Peter presented me with a new trike. It wasn't that it was brand new – well, the rear axle was brand new, having been shipped from the UK – but the bike frame was one that had been used by Sara Carrigan at the 2004 Athens Olympics, where she had won gold in the road race. I figured this was a fantastic omen. This trike was 8 kgs lighter than my red, steel-framed trike and I was now 12 kgs lighter than I had been in Denmark. When I rode

Chapter 10: Discovering Gold

it I felt like I was flying. The test was going to be when I met up with competitors in Europe to see if it had all paid off. That week at the training camp, our head coach, Peter, said 'Train with a sense of purpose and finish with a sense of achievement. Crunch time is everyday'. This statement is so true, as each individual has to realise that having self-confidence is only one aspect of the journey; responsibility is the other. Only when you are willing to be fully responsible for yourself will you be truly confident in your efforts.

I'm happy to say that, in the long run, trying to discover my own pot of gold definitely paid off. That June, we spent time in France and Spain, where I had some mixed results with some wins and some second places. I had learnt enough from the previous year of what I had to do to be competitive. By putting all those lessons into something tangible, 2012 culminated in *Discovering Gold* when I won the gold medal in the time trial at the London Paralympics.

There are times when you feel you are making the same mistakes. This is when you really need to focus on causation and discover what lessons your mistakes hold. Is the environment wrong? Are your relationships wrong? Is your approach wrong? If any of these areas have a problem you will not reach that pot of gold.

Your mistakes will help you identify the problem. They will show you what your strengths and weaknesses are. Knowing what your strengths and weaknesses are will help you focus on the areas that you need to focus on. By acknowledging your weaknesses and how they are going to affect your performance you can effectively address them and spend more quality time working on those areas. If you try to justify them or make excuses you will never reach that 'pot of gold'. But whatever you do don't obsess about your mistakes or over-think what needs to be done. For me it was very simple, lose weight and get fitter. I like to use the KISS principle: *Keep It Simple, Stupid*. Don't over-complicate things.

There are many ways to start helping yourself. The first thing you can do is to write down a hurdle in your life then write different ways of getting around it.

You can also make a list of things that may have derailed you in reaching a goal. By knowing what has pushed us off our path we can turn that around. List what has helped you get through that weakness or hurdle and the ways you did it in the past.

Each day, look back at yesterday and ask yourself, 'What worked and what didn't?' It doesn't have to be anything specific that you were trying to accomplish, but the more we teach ourselves to look at our mistakes the better we get at learning how to change things.

> 'Learn what helps you, what holds you back, what makes you more effective and what slows you down. Learn from your encounters, your experiences, your joys, your setbacks and from the surprising twists that life often takes. In everything is the valuable opportunity to learn if you'll simply decide to do so. Learn from it all, and make each day better than the one before.'
> **– Ralph S. Marston Jr**

Chapter 10: Discovering Gold

As you will have been able to tell, I am a great believer in writing things down. It makes them real. By making a list of things that may have derailed you in the past, you will discover what they are so that you can stop them from happening again. That way, you will be able to reach your goal and your own pot of gold.

Lastly, think about past habits that have helped you towards a goal, then try to put them in place in order to help you through to a new goal. It is very important to sit down and note what helped in the past.

Finding your own pot of gold isn't that hard; it's just about a shift in the way you think and persevere. Start realising that mistakes can be good to learn from. Learn from those mistakes, change the way you tackle things and really start to believe in yourself, because your beliefs can really limit the discovery of your gold!

Chapter 11:
Living Now

Most people plan for the future, worry about what they've done wrong in the past, but forget about living in the now. We get distracted with yesterday and tomorrow and end up missing amazing moments that are right here in front of us in the present. This chapter, 'Living Now', is all about focusing on the present and making it the best it can be.

There are a number of benefits to living in the present. Too often we worry about what we might have done or said in the past and beat ourselves up about mistakes we have made. If you stop worrying about the past and the future, you will start living in the present and living in acceptance. You must realise you can't change the past and have no idea what the future will bring. It doesn't exist, so start living for today.

Living right now will have a huge impact on your life. By ceasing all unnecessary worries about the past or future, you will become more creative and efficient. If you think about living now, rather than what you will be doing tomorrow, you will become more efficient at everything you do. It will also help improve your concentration; you may start noticing life around you in the here and now, instead of obsessing about what life will be like a day, month or year from now.

Living in the now is also excellent for your health. If you aren't stressed about the mistakes you have made in the past, or worried about what you will be doing in the future, you can better relax.

> 'The secret of health for both mind and body is not to mourn for the past or worry about the future, but to live in the present moment wisely and earnestly.'
> **– Buddha**

A 2009 study by Matthew Killingsworth and Daniel Gilbert at Harvard University found that 46% of people spend nearly half their time thinking about something other than what they were actually doing. We all do it, think about other things while we are doing something else. We like to call it multi-tasking. But if we stop the chatter inside our own heads we will get through things much quicker and more efficiently.

Those who live in the present are surprised how much they pick up that they might otherwise have missed. If we worry about what might or might not happen in the future we will miss potentially life-changing opportunities.

> 'If you worry about what might be and wonder what might have been, you will ignore what is.'
> **– Unknown**

I do a lot of public speaking to schools, corporations, sport clubs and community groups and one of the most interesting questions I have ever been asked came from a 9 year old. She asked 'If you could go back in history and change your diagnosis of MS, would you?' Amazing how we get the best questions from the youngest people! But it really made me think. Would I change my diagnosis if I could? The simple answer is *no*. Things happen to us for a reason and, to live in the now, we must accept things, not dwell on what-ifs.

Chapter 11: Living Now

My diagnosis made me who I am today. I guess I can look back and say I was a good person and liked myself before my diagnosis. But if I am truly honest with myself I like who I am now better than the person I was before. Multiple Sclerosis has made me who I am today and given me opportunities that I never would have had. I think that it has made me more empathetic towards people and more understanding of their hardships. It has also made me a more determined person. Not that I wasn't before, but I now channel my determination into trying to make things better for others.

My diagnosis has given me the opportunity to become an Ambassador for MS; to educate, motivate and advocate. It has also given me the opportunity to be an elite athlete again, later in life than most, in two sports. My diagnosis has given me the opportunity to compete around the world at the Paralympics, World Cups and World Championships. It has also given me the chance to found the 24 Hour Mega Swim and raise money for people living with MS. Without my diagnosis, none of this would have happened in my life.

Each morning when I wake up, I don't think 'What if I had never been diagnosed? What would I be doing today?' That would be living in the past and I am happier to live in the now. I can't say I only live in the moment. We often brag that we can multi-task and, in that respect, I am no different to anyone else. We believe it is fantastic to be able to do this because we are living in an 'instant' society. But by trying to do one thing and thinking about another we don't live in the present. It is hard to quiet your mind, so don't try to stop your thoughts; just stop doing two, three or four things at the same time. Accept what is happening right now as the only thing that is important. That way, you will accept your life as it is right at this very moment. By thinking or living in the past or future you give up your personal power to decide right now what is best for you. Create the best life possible by not worrying about the past or future.

The big question is: how do we live in the present? Take the time to look at how you do things in life. If you are a multi-tasker, stop and start to do things one at a time. If you are speaking on the phone then just do that; don't write while speaking. If you are speaking to someone face to face, don't think about what you have to do later that day. *Really* listen to the person you are speaking to. Be engaged in the conversation, not the thoughts going through your head. You will actually start to enjoy speaking with your friends and acquaintances because you will be engaged in the conversation.

If you tend to do other tasks while you are eating then stop. Just have your breakfast, lunch or dinner. Start enjoying the food that you are eating, taste the food, feel the texture, enjoy the aromas and savour each mouthful. When you are driving, don't do anything else but drive. We have all seen those who think that it is a good thing to multi-task while driving – women putting on their makeup, people texting or some even reading. Be in the present while you are doing these things.

Don't try to do too much. Make a list of what needs doing. Rank the items in order of priority and then tick them off as you complete them. If you try to do your tasks all together or a few at a time you won't complete them properly and will be rushing to get things done. Take your time. As my

Chapter 11: Living Now

dad used to say to me: 'Rome wasn't built in a day. Why are you rushing?' When you finish the first item on your list, take some time. Think about your next task and how you will tackle it. Taking your time is not a crime!

During each day, take some time for just you, even if it is only five or ten minutes. Everyone can find that time; there are no excuses. Sit quietly and think about how you are breathing. Look around you and notice the world. Try to be comfortable about being just in that moment. There are so many ways to help you do this.

I recommend using an app called *Smiling Mind*. There are many tools to assist us out there. This app is free and requires nothing from you but your ability to listen. It will give you that five or ten minutes you need to be mindful and in the present.

Stop worrying about the future. It is okay to plan, but be prepared to change those plans if something unanticipated happens. In the present, we have no idea what the future will hold, so it is important not to worry about it. By worrying, you give up your personal power and are living for something that hasn't happened yet. I hate the fact that people make New Year's Resolutions.

In the lead up to New Year's Eve people talk about what their resolutions will be. Why not start in the present? If you want to change something, do it now. Don't wait for a magical date that you think will make it happen.

When you are always living for the future and what it may hold you will miss the immediate reality of what is happening right now. You will miss opportunities that may present themselves. I watched a YouTube video by Eckhart Toole. Eckhart is a German-born author and Canadian resident. In 2011, he was listed in the Watkins Review as the most spiritually influential person in the world. In his video, he says people live as if the present moment were an obstacle that needs to be overcome in order to get to some elusive better place that will never arrive. This is so true and it certainly makes living very hard. If you make now the primary focus of your life you will be amazed what possibilities will open up. You can make brief visits to the past because that is how we learn, from our mistakes, but don't fret about past mistakes; just learn and move on.

Being mindful and in the present is hard to do. The best thing you can do is to keep practicing. It certainly won't happen overnight, but you will get better at it. If you can start by just trying then you are halfway there.

When I decided to try my hand at cycling I went up to my first Australian National Para-Cycling Championships in Queensland in 2011 with no idea of what the future would hold. I just wanted to go up and ride, be in the moment and not even think about 'what if?' I didn't even look at the qualifying speeds for the national team. I didn't want to think of 'what might be'; I just wanted to enjoy riding around the Glass House Mountains and concentrate on climbing the hills.

I honestly believe I did so well because I just went out and enjoyed what I was doing. I wasn't worried about what the future held. It was just about riding. There was no pressure; there was only enjoyment. As it turned out, I absolutely

Chapter 11: Living Now

smashed the average speed required on the trike to make the national team. Our head coach was surprised I didn't even know what the qualifying speed was.

The problem now for me is that I am a numbers person. I am always looking at what others are doing. I compare myself with my competitors, then think about the future and how I will race them. It's okay to plan, but I find I must really practice mindfulness whenever I start obsessing. This doesn't mean that I can't use the data I have collected on my competitors to aim for where I would like to be. I can live in the present and adjust what I do to stay on target. It is okay for me to look at ways to improve what I am doing today in my training to make me stronger and fitter for the future.

Living in the past is just as bad as trying to live for the future. How many times have we said something we later regretted or held a grudge because someone spoke ill of us? We certainly can't go back in time – if you can, could you please share your secret with me? We must learn to let the things we can't change fade away. Forget about what may have been said in anger. Forgive people and let go of grudges. Life is definitely too short for any of that.

It happens all the time. Someone will ask what the best time of your life was, but how do you know? Instead of thinking of 'better times' or wishing you could have more of what happened last year, you can be enjoying the best time of your life right now! Make each day the best ever. During my talks, I always say that you should live life as though you have a terminal illness. Most people think I am nuts, but if you look at life this way you will live it with all the passion it ought to be lived with!

Here are some ideas to take away:
- Take 5–10 minutes each day to sit quietly and really take in all things around you.

- Make a list of things you want to accomplish that day and work through them, one task at a time.

- Wake every morning with a smile. Envisage a great day about to unfold and remind yourself how truly blessed you are to be alive, and to be living a life that has limitless possibilities.

Chapter 12:
Powerful Belief

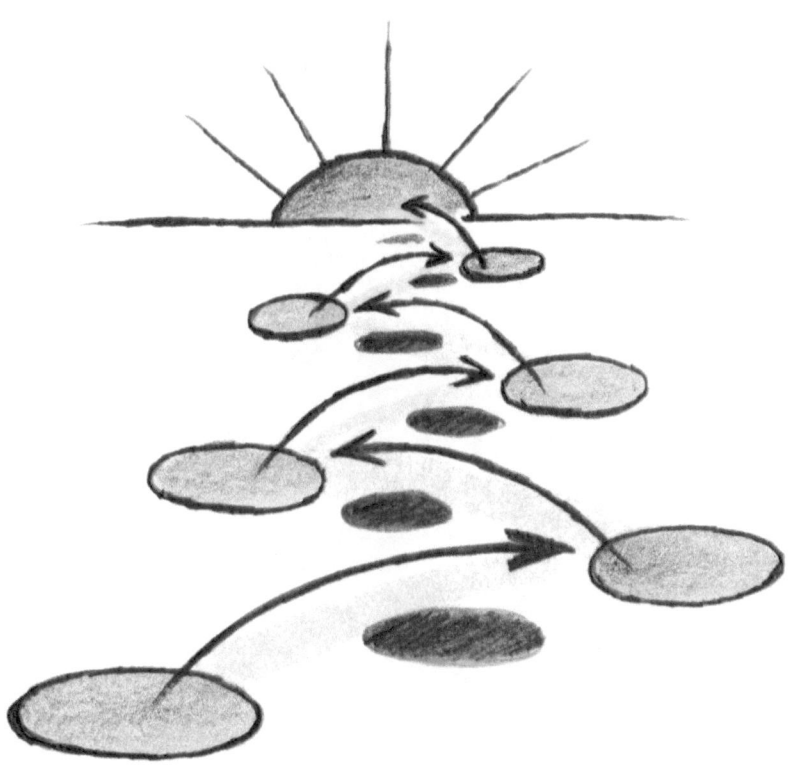

Throughout the years, I have had negative people in my life who were quick to cut me down. Fortunately, I have been able to believe in myself and in my abilities, and forge ahead no matter what those critics said. Powerful belief is about having faith in your abilities and believing that you can accomplish anything you put your mind to. But belief is not all it takes. You must put actions into your beliefs in order for your goals and dreams to come to fruition. If you want to be a millionaire, no one is going to just give you the money. You will have to earn it, so set the steps in place to get to that goal.

Having self-belief gives you the power to accomplish anything. When starting something new, you must tell yourself that it will be great. You may not believe this at the start, but if you keep saying it – not only in your head, but also aloud – then eventually you will believe.

When you believe you are something, you embody and embrace it. If you think that you will be bad at doing something, then you most likely will be. But if you go in with a patient, open mindset, you will likely find eventual success. If there is a negative spin on your change or action, negativity will flow through into the task at hand.

Believing in yourself equals success, but failing can also help you succeed. Without the odd failure, you won't have or appreciate success. When trying something new, you have to expect some failures. Try to look at them as temporary setbacks. This will show you why and how to move forward towards the success you are due. Your self-belief will strengthen as you succeed.

If you believe in yourself, your goals and dreams become reality. It is hard to keep those positive beliefs going because there will be people around who will react negatively to what you are attempting to do. That is why it is important to surround yourself with positive people. I have pushed the negative people in my life to the side. They may be friends, but I keep my contact with them to a minimum. As much as you want to change people's mindsets, some will always look at life in a negative light. We all know them; they are the people my mum used to say 'Woke up on the wrong side of the bed'. Nothing is good in their lives (or so they think) and they are fatalistic by nature. You can defend yourself from negativity if you believe in yourself and what you want to accomplish.

If you don't believe in yourself your self-doubt will devour your confidence and strip logic and reason from your mindset. Self-doubt is about perspective. We become so complacent with where we are at right now that any change or hurdle debilitates us. We have to change the way we see things, put a different perspective on it and think of all the good and positive outcomes we will experience in the future. We often have a negative perspective drummed into us, so start to believe it. We must give ourselves permission to believe in a positive outcome. When you were born you didn't have any beliefs; it is only through social conditioning that self-doubt enters our lives.

I think back to that 10 year old who so wanted to be an

Chapter 12: Powerful Belief

Olympic gymnast. I had the belief that I could do this. However, I was told right from the start that I was too fat and would never get there. What a way to teach a child about believing in themselves! It would have been better to take me aside and say something like 'Your body type just isn't right for gymnastics. What other sport do you like?' Giving me another option to think about would have put a positive spin on my situation. As it was, I'm at least grateful I had parents who kept me involved in other sports, for that is when swimming came into my life.

As a swimmer, I never felt anything was impossible. The coaches I had throughout that career asked me what my goals were and guided me towards them by believing in my abilities. This translated into my belief that one day I could attain whatever goal I set. I was lucky to have had the mentors I have had.

Funnily enough, things seemed to revert to those early 'gymnastics years' when, in 2007, after rowing in my first-ever nationals and winning the LTA (Legs, Trunk and Arms) double scull, I was told I would never be a good enough rower to make a national team, or ever think of representing Australia. There I was, thirty-six years later, on the receiving end of the same negativity. At least this time I was old enough to believe in myself and prove a point to the people who had doubted me. I don't think they realised what a pigheaded and stubborn person they were dealing with. I was someone who fiercely believed in herself.

Even the neurologist who diagnosed me with Multiple Sclerosis spoke in the negative when he said 'Your life as you know it is over. You will never do this sport stuff again.'

He was right: my life as I knew it *was* over, but not in a negative way. Sure, in the beginning, I was very down and thought negatively. It took not only my family and friends talking positively, but my own self-belief to realise that my life was over as I knew it, but in a positive way!

If I had never been diagnosed with MS, my life would never have had so many amazing possibilities opened up to me:

- I would never have become a rower – or a cyclist for that matter.

- I would never have started the 24 Hour Mega Swim and raised millions of dollars.

- The Go for Gold Scholarships for people living with MS would not be up and running.

- I would never have gone to the Paralympics and come home with a gold medal.

- I certainly wouldn't be travelling the world on a national team competing internationally.

- I wouldn't have met all the wonderful people who I now call friends, and …

- I probably wouldn't be writing this book!

It all comes down to the self-belief. After my diagnosis, I could have just curled up in a ball and given up. If I had done that, I would probably be in a wheelchair full-time, with my MS progressing. In retrospect, it was probably the best thing that neurologist could have said to pigheaded, stubborn me. He spurred me on, his words like a red flag to a bull. I wasn't going to let my MS define who I was. I'm lucky I had belief in myself, where others might not have.

When I started racing as a Para-cyclist, I even had another rider speak to me negatively, which almost crushed my self-belief. It was my first World Cup in Sydney in 2011 and I really had no idea what I was doing. I really knew nothing about cycle racing, so decided that I would just go out and ride as hard as I could.

The night before the road race, a teammate asked me how I was going to race the road race. I laughed and said I had no idea, but that the Men's World Champion, David Stone, was racing as well, so I figured I would just try to follow him, try to stick to him like glue. I thought that would be a good tactic! The other rider laughed and said 'Carol, he's a real athlete.' That comment stunned me; it was like being hit in the guts. I couldn't understand how a teammate could be so negative. Yes, I was new to cycling, and I was much heavier than I am now and certainly not as fit as I could have been, but that night, as I tried to sleep, all I could think was *Maybe she's right. What am I doing here?* I had to do some serious self-talking to get that negative feeling out of me. I don't know if she even knew what she had said, or how devastating it could have been.

The next day, as we lined up at the start of the race, I was right next to David Stone and, as we headed off, I put my plan into action and stayed with him for as long as I could

… which wasn't very long! But that didn't dissuade me; I just worked with a couple of the other riders for the entire race. I ended up being the first woman across the line and won my first international road race that day. Sure, there was only one other woman in the race, from South Africa, but that didn't matter to me. I had actually beaten some of the guys. I had given it my all and took back my self-belief at the same time.

I was able to use that self-belief the following year at the Paralympics, where I had to race the men in the time trial. David Stone started one minute behind me and my goal was to stay in front of him to a certain point on the course. When that point came and went without him passing me, I was over the moon and knew I was having a great race. As it turned out, I won the gold and David won the bronze. At that point, those words came back to me: 'he's a real athlete' and I realised that I could positively say at that point: '*I* am a real athlete!'

We are born without any beliefs and it is only through the process of growing up that our beliefs are created and become learned behaviours. These beliefs are learnt from our parents, siblings, teachers, friends and mentors. They are also learnt from our past experiences. As small children, we think we can do anything, so where does that go as we grow up? As young people, teens to adulthood, we think we are invincible, which can be good and bad. It's good because we will try anything and believe we can do anything, but it's bad because sometimes, at that age, we tend not to think of the consequences of the dangerous things we attempt. As we age, I think that we start believing the doubt around us and this, in turn, leads us to question our beliefs. If we

Chapter 12: Powerful Belief

have someone telling us that we aren't going to be able to do something, or won't be good at it, we stop ourselves from experiencing things that could be incredible.

I often ask groups I am speaking to 'What would you attempt to do if you knew you couldn't fail?' Not all of us are going to be the best in the world, nor the smartest or fastest, but that shouldn't stop us from trying things that we may really end up enjoying, whether good at it or not.

How do you learn self-belief? It takes time, but you can do it. Start with taking any negative belief about yourself and try looking at it in a positive way. My pigheaded and stubbornness can be perceived as determination. I have always been determined to live life the way I want to. As a kid, that stubbornness got me into a bit of trouble, but has kept me in good stead as I have dealt with the challenges in my life. Always try to put a positive spin on that negative thought.

There are ways to help you develop powerful self-belief everyday. I think some of the best ideas come from Mark Tyrell, a therapist and co-founder of Uncommon Knowledge. He talks about thinking about your favourite superheroes, taking yourself back to your childhood. If your belief is waning, what would your superhero do? Prime your mind with those qualities and positive characteristics because this will help determine your behaviour. As he says: 'Not that you'll start flying to the rescue of stranded citizens, but the pattern of superhero powers is one of ability, courage and competence.'

To help yourself with that powerful belief, write down

positive characteristics every day. These characteristics don't have to relate to you; just try to come up with positive characteristics, such as: intelligent, generous, sexy, strong, humorous, approachable, determined and popular. Try to come up with more words each day. Focus on the words. Learn to embrace them, read them often and your subconscious will start to embrace them as well. It is amazing how you will start to take on those qualities.

There are times even during a race when I do a lot of self-coaching and motivating. It's as if I was talking to someone else. If my brain starts thinking things like 'wow, this is too hard', 'I'm not feeling great', or any general type of negative thought, I talk to myself like I'm spurring someone else on, being positive and motivational to get past those negativities. Again it takes practice to be able to do this, so no matter what you are facing try to motivate yourself the way someone else might.

No matter how you try to increase your belief you really have to develop a vision of what you believe you can do or be. Like I have done with sport and visualising the outcome of my swimming, rowing or cycling race, it is important to do the same thing to visualise yourself as a person who has amazing self-belief and success. The more you practice this, the more you will start to really believe in yourself.

Practicing all this and learning to believe in yourself doesn't mean you will be perfect. None of us are. We all have faults we must realise. But having powerful belief in yourself will give you permission to make mistakes and be able to deal with setbacks, which are not the end of the world. Those setbacks will help you move forward and, with that, your

Chapter 12: Powerful Belief

self-belief grows and the people around you believe in you as well.

Even though I have very powerful belief in myself now, it has not happened overnight. I have still had to learn how to increase that belief over the years and I have known people who have unknowingly helped me do that. There were times towards the end of my rowing career when the head coach put negative thoughts into my head. The difference when I switched to cycling was incredible. With positive people involved in Para-cycling within the coaching fraternity, it turned my beliefs around and certainly helped me get to where I have. It has also made me realise that I have more to give this sport and, with that powerful belief, I will continue on this amazing journey.

Chapter 13:
Celebrate Success

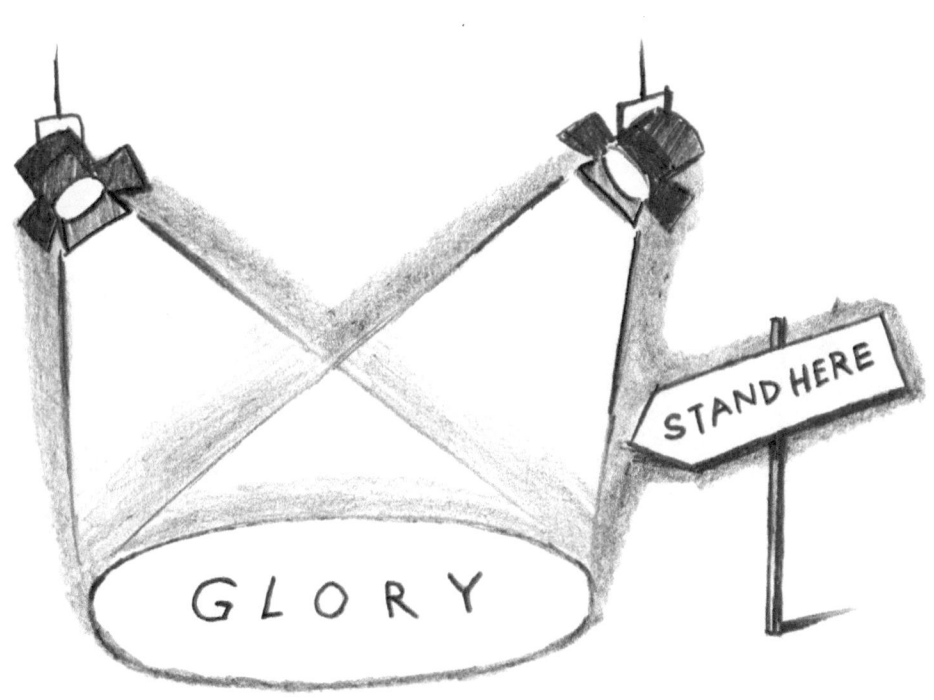

It's important to celebrate your successes. Not just the big goals you have set for yourself, but also the little goals and steps along the way. Celebrating these successes is important and good for you because it reminds you of the reasons you set your goal in the first place.

Celebrating success is about acknowledging what you have achieved. It is about remembering all the hard work you and everyone else have put into achieving your goal. It is a way to reinforce your behaviour in how you reached your success. It's hard to actually teach people how to celebrate because there are so many different ideas of celebration. For some, it is an unassuming affair, but for others it is pomp and circumstance. Failing to celebrate your success neglects the fact that you have succeeded.

Success breeds success, so it is important to celebrate and acknowledge that you have accomplished what you set out to do. It is important to celebrate even your stepping stone goals and your minor successes, as it will keep you motivated and committed to remain on track for your ultimate goal. It will also remind you how far you have come and the challenges you have met. It will start changing your attitude by telling you that you have already succeeded. These are the little goals you put in your planning days, months or even years before.

Celebrating these goals keeps your team together: your coaches, mentors, family, friends or work colleagues, if your goal centres around your business or employment. It is important to make sure they are included because no one can be successful on their own. There is always some sort of team surrounding you, whether your success is work, sport or life-related. Sharing a celebration of your accomplishments, no matter how small, helps your team bond together. It also helps everyone remember what you need to accomplish in order to have further celebrations in the future. People always want to be part of a winning team and celebrating will keep your entire 'team' engaged and working with you to repeat those successes.

When first putting your goals in place, remember to put some type of celebration plans in for when you reach your stepping stone or minor goal. These can be anything that you want, but they should be included in your written plans from the outset. You might purchase yourself something that you have always wanted, or treat yourself to a bit of chocolate or a dinner out. Acknowledge what you have accomplished; this will motivate you to take the next step.

Celebrating your success will help validate your accomplishment and make it memorable. I have had a number of successes throughout my life, through my policing, business and athletic careers. They have all been celebrated very differently, but I certainly remember most of them.

During my policing career, I had a number of reasons to celebrate: the first being getting through the police college to become an officer. I celebrated this milestone with my family. We celebrated the fact I was carrying on a family tradition. It was a celebration to congratulate me, but the

Chapter 13: Celebrate Success

family connotation was most important. I think my dad was happier about the celebration than I was because his daughter was following in his footsteps. But that was what it was all about: celebrating that family tradition.

During my years in the Morality Bureau, (which is just a nice name for the Vice Squad), I worked in both the prostitution and drug sections. After a project we'd worked on for months wrapped up, with arrests and crucial paperwork done, it would be time to celebrate our success. This usually consisted of a number of alcoholic beverages consumed either at a local bar or, if it was the middle of the night, in the underground car park of our office building.

As far as we were concerned anywhere was good to celebrate! I am very happy to say that my ways have changed since that type of celebrating thirty years ago now! It was our way of letting our hair down and working out the stresses of the night, and also an acknowledgement of a job well done. There were times when we would also celebrate after a court case had run its course. We would either be celebrating a good outcome or commiserating the fact we weren't able to get a conviction. (Which, I am happy to say, didn't happen very often!)

I guess my final celebration on the police force was when I had decided to leave the department and move to Australia. This celebration was about thanking the family, friends and colleagues who had stood by me for fourteen years. It was a mix of emotions: one of which was a tinge of sadness because I was moving 16,000 kms away to another country. However, it was also a celebration of a new start: a completely new way of life in a different country.

When I first arrived in Australia, I worked for Australia Post in a number of different capacities. At one point, I was the Delivery Manager of a local post office in the north of Melbourne. I had gone into the position after a manager had been stood down and the staff weren't too happy about it. The office was the worst-performing office in the district and I was asked to try to rectify that. So I went into the job somewhat apprehensive but, by putting some plans in place and jumping in to help the staff out myself, I started to see improvements. One of the things I put in place was an employee of the month program. The staff could gain or lose points for certain things during the course of the day. At the end of the month, the employee with the most points would get two tickets to the movies, but, more importantly, I would buy lunch for the entire group. I always made sure this was on the last Friday of every month. It seemed that on this day our sick leave was at its highest, so by purchasing the staff lunch they all turned up.

As we started to rise in the rankings within the district, I would hold special days with breakfast provided or a more upmarket lunch. It was my way of showing the staff that it was okay to celebrate these little steps and, more importantly, it was my way of saying thank you. We certainly weren't the best or top office, but there was significant improvement, which was important to celebrate. It made the staff more motivated and helped them believe that they had achieved something. Whether it was conscious strategy or not, it worked!

The London Paralympics were a different type of celebrating altogether, one that seemed to go on and on. Celebrating the winning of a Paralympic gold medal starts with meeting

Chapter 13: Celebrate Success

the other athletes in the medal presentation area. For me, it was amazing when both my competitors grabbed me in a big hug and congratulated me. I had to race the men and it interested me to see how they would react. I was pleasantly surprised. I don't know why I would have thought any differently, as they are amazing competitors, but they were genuinely happy for me.

From there you have the formal medal presentation and are given a rundown of what will take place, where you should move to and when to step up to receive your medal. All the while the crowd is cheering and I can see my family at the fence. All I wanted was to run over and hug them! Once the formal presentation and media requests for photos were completed, I was finally able to go to my family. My sister had the widest smile on her face that I had ever seen. When I hugged her she burst into tears. My mom and aunt were so excited. It was great to be able to hug them and have photos together. But my Paralympic campaign was far from over, as there was still one race to go in two days' time. It was important not to be too carried away with any type of celebration.

When I arrived back at the village, there were more quasi-celebrations with teammates and then, the next day, at last, I was able to have a celebratory lunch with family. But celebrating with my family over lunch, and with my medal, brought our special gathering into the public arena, where everyone around us in the restaurant wanted photos with my medal. It was like being an instant celebrity, even though none of them knew who I was or what sport I played!

The celebrations didn't end there, even after racing the

road race a couple of days later. The Closing Ceremonies were a way for all the athletes, coaches and support staff to celebrate, no matter how well we had done. It was an amazing experience, standing on the field of the stadium with the crowd cheering all around us. To be honest, the night went by in a blur. We then celebrated after the Closing Ceremonies with the Brits and the Canadians (I guess you could call it the Commonwealth celebrations!). This was a celebration of years of hard work to get where we were and there were certainly a few athletes 'letting their hair down'! Even on our flight home, a chartered Qantas flight just for us, the celebrations continued. Upon our arrival into Sydney, we were met by the country's top politicians for a huge welcome home, with some of the athletes' families there as well as the media. It felt like a week of non-stop celebration. I was looking forward to getting home to hide and rest for at least a day.

It was amazing, but the celebrations continued once I was home. They had to. I had so many people to thank who had supported me in this campaign – my coach, my friends, the Victorian Institute of Sport staff and family – and it was important that they get a chance to hold onto or wear my medal. For me, the most important thing is to make sure those who have stood by you and helped are properly thanked. We can't get to this point without assistance, so never forget those people.

Some people feel self-conscious about celebrating their successes because they feel it is a form of bragging. But you should be proud of yourself and your accomplishments and share it, just as long as it is done the right way. Don't brag to the point that you feel you are better than others,

Chapter 13: Celebrate Success

but it is okay to be proud and, in this day and age, it is okay to share your successes on social media, or on a blog you may be writing. If you are worried that certain friends will think that you are big-noting yourself by being proud of your accomplishments then those people may not be true friends. As long as you have included your friends in your celebrations then they will be just as proud of you as you are of yourself.

The ongoing celebrations at home became public motivation to ask 'what's next?' I knew I had to take a break and try to see what a normal life was like. But it was always in the back of my mind: *How can I top a gold Paralympic medal?* There is a quote by Mia Hamm: 'Celebrate what you've accomplished, but raise the bar a little higher each time you succeed.'

I think that even though I was very proud of myself for winning my gold medal, there was always a little voice in the back of my head wondering if I truly deserved it. I say this because my main competitor, Marie-Eve, didn't race and she had beaten me the year before. I wondered whether I still would've won if she had raced. I knew that this shouldn't matter – she hadn't raced and I had – but it was there in my head. So it was easy to raise the bar by focusing on winning the World Championships the following year. Winning in London had motivated me to do even better the following year. This is what is meant by 'Success breeds success'. I became more committed being out there, working on my weaknesses so that I could improve even more.

But what is success? It's different for everyone. I have been lucky in that my successes have meant coming home with gold medals. But even if I didn't win those gold medals, I believe I would have still come home thinking that I had been successful because I knew that I had done everything in my power to be the best I could be. In London, for example, I had nothing left to give at the end of my time trial. If I had come last, I would have still been successful and would have accepted that the others were just faster than me. I would have also been celebrating the fact that almost forty-one years after dreaming of going to the Olympics as a 9-year-old, I could actually celebrate making the team. My dream had come true. If I came home without a medal I would have still been motivated to improve and keep trying for that win the following year.

Every year when my racing season is over I make sure that I set aside some time just for Russ and myself. For the last couple of years, this has meant going away for a few days. It never had to be for long, but it has always been more about the quality than the quantity of the time we spent together, away from our real world and spoiling ourselves at the same time. He is a big part of my team and what he brings to my team allows me to spend the time training. Without him, it would be extremely hard to do what I do. He is also the one who can look at me and tell me to slow down or go rest. After twenty years, he knows when I need to do this. So we always do something special to recharge and celebrate the year that was. This is my way of thanking him for everything he brings to my life.

So what can we do to learn to celebrate our successes?

- Every night, as you are going to bed, write down what your successes of the day were. They don't have to be huge; just put down the little successes you have had during the day. This way, you go to

Chapter 13: Celebrate Success

sleep successful and wake up a success! If, after a week or two, you can say you have had at least one small success a day then celebrate that fact. It doesn't have to be anything huge; it could just be putting aside time for yourself.

- When writing down your steps and goals make sure you include the things you will do to celebrate. Make them real by writing them down and then make sure that you actually do the celebrating. If you fail to celebrate the small steps and constantly think about the end goal, you will always be focused on what you haven't accomplished rather than what you have.

- If you know of someone who is also trying to accomplish a goal, support them. By supporting them and their successes, you will find yourself surrounded by others who are successful. Help them celebrate, to see this can motivate you to celebrate your own successes.

- Make to-do lists each day and, as you cross off what you have accomplished, make sure you realise that this is a form of success. This will help your realise how successful you are on a daily basis.

- Sit and make a list of all the things you have achieved in your life that you are proud of. Look at this list as if you were someone else. This will help you realise the success you have had, instead of focusing on what you haven't accomplished. If you can read this list and smile, then do something to celebrate!

'Stop worrying about the potholes in the road and celebrate the journey.'
  – Fitzhugh Mullan M.D. (Professor of Paediatrics and Public Health at George Washington University)

Make sure you 'celebrate the journey' as you are travelling it.

Afterword

I have been lucky in the fact that for most of my life I have been pretty sure of myself and had the belief that I could do anything I put my mind to. I am sure that this has been instilled in me at a young age through the family I was lucky enough to be a part of and through the number of coaches/mentors I have had throughout the years. Other than a few 'bumps' in the road of life I have had so many awesome journeys and I believe and look forward to the many more that I am sure will come my way. I have learnt to not fear that 'bump' in the road but to plow right through and accept any changes or challenges that may come my way, whether they be good or bad.

Being diagnosed with Multiple Sclerosis was probably a blessing in disguise. It made me realise that life is very short and instead of stressing out about how much money I was making or high up the line of command I could go with work, it was time to stop, look around and enjoy life. It also helped me understand that it is important that you don't 'live to work' but instead 'work to live'. I realised that I would get by in life without those stresses, without having the best of everything and without climbing that corporate ladder. Not that it is wrong for everyone but for me MS was a wake up call that told me to 'Live My Life' and try to give back a bit more to others.

I really do hope that after reading my book it has inspired you to look deep within your heart to find what you believe your inner gold to be and to embrace any change that comes your way, give your fear of the unknown a kick up the butt! Wake up each morning and say to yourself 'What would I attempt to do today if I knew I couldn't fail?' Then go out and do whatever it is, enjoy the challenge and you will most likely love the outcome no matter how good or bad you are at it. Don't just not attempt something out of fear, remember that 80% of something is better than 100% of nothing.

I have learnt a lot of lessons on my journey of living my life with Multiple Sclerosis through friends, family and mentors and would like to leave you with just a few:

1. Dare to face your fears and believe in yourself and you can accomplish anything.

2. To love the journey and not the destination because today is not a dress rehearsal, today is the only guarantee you get.

3. Don't judge a book by it's cover – your perceived idea of what someone can do may be completely wrong.

4. See every difficulty as a challenge, a stepping stone and never be defeated by anything or anyone.

5. Take two words out of your vocabulary: can't and never.

6. Always DREAM BIG!

About Carol

A sports fanatic, workaholic, former undercover police officer and Multiple Sclerosis advocate, Carol Cooke is one of the most inspirational figures in Australian sport.

Carol was born in Canada in 1961. She worked as a police officer in Canada for 14 years including 4 years undercover with the drug and prostitution squads. Carol moved to Australia for love and was devastated when diagnosed with Multiple Sclerosis in 1998 only 3 years into her marriage. Told that she would never work again or compete in sport, she was advised she should put her affairs in order before she became incapacitated. She defied the odds. By 2001 she was using a wheelchair full time. However, through regular exercise and Botox injections in her legs, Carol not only walks but rows and cycles at an international level.

Carol was a former national level swimmer in Canada, with a goal of going to the 1980 Olympics; the opportunity vanished with the Moscow Games being boycotted. In 2006 she took up rowing, having been identified at an Australian Paralympic Talent Search day. She proved a natural on the water narrowly missing out on a position on the Beijing 2008 team and placed sixth at the 2009 World Rowing Championships.

Carol switched sports to cycling with a plan to make the London 2012 Paralympic team. In 2011 she made the Australian team for the UCI Para Cycling World Championships. Carol made the impact she had desired claiming silver in both the Road Race and Time Trial. Her form flowed through to the 2012 Australian National Road Championships. Carol achieved her goal when she was named in the Australian Paralympic team for London 2012. In London years of toil paid off. Carol won a gold medal in the Mixed Time Trial T1-T2 event. Carol went on to win 5 World Championships, 3 in the Time Trial and 2 in the Road Race. She made the team for the 2016 Rio Paralympics and came home with 2 gold medals.

Since being diagnosed with Multiple Sclerosis, Carol has dedicated her working life to raising awareness and funds for MS. She developed and still leads the operation of the 24 Hour Mega Swim event, dedicated to raising money for MS. The project has now expanded to run in four states across 17 events and raised in excess of $7.4 million since 2001.

Carol lives with the philosophy that you must dare to face your fears. She has come through adversity and change with persistence and an incredible mindset. It is advice she shares through her work as an inspiring motivational speaker telling of her incredible life story.

Email for Enquiries and Availability
Carol's Speaker Bio

Carol Cooke AM

Carol was born in Canada in 1961. She worked as a police officer in Canada for 14 years, including 4 years undercover with the drug squad. Carol was devastated when diagnosed with Multiple Sclerosis in 1998. By 2001, she was using a wheelchair full-time. However, through regular exercise and Botox injections in her legs, Carol not only regained the ability to walk, but took up competitive rowing and cycling.

Carol was a former national swimmer in Canada. In 2006, she took up rowing, having been identified at a Paralympic Talent Search Day. She proved a natural on the water, narrowly missing out on a position on the Beijing 2008 team but placing sixth at the 2009 World Rowing Championships.

Carol switched sports to cycling with a plan to make the London 2012 Paralympic team. Carol achieved her goal when she was named in the Australian Paralympic team for London 2012.

In London, years of toil paid off. Carol won a gold medal in the Mixed Time Trial T1-2 event. In 2013 at the World Para Cycling Championships, Carol became a Dual World Champion and backed it up in 2014.

Since being diagnosed with Multiple Sclerosis, Carol has dedicated her working life to raising awareness and funds for MS.

She developed and still leads the operation of the 24 Hour Mega Swim event, dedicated to raising money for MS. In 2014, Carol was honoured with an Australia Day Award which named her a 'Member' of the Order of Australia (AM) for her service to sport and philanthropy.

Carol lives the philosophy that you must dare to face your fears and believe in yourself. She says that you have to have the Courage to take a Chance to make a Change. It is advice she shares through her work as an inspiring motivational speaker telling of her incredible life story and through her book *Cycle of Life – a Gold Medal Paralympian's Secrets to Success*.

Contact Details

Phone: 0417 360 883
Email: carol@carolcooke.com.au
Web: www.carolcooke.com.au

Carol is also on the following speakers websites:

http://www.keynoteentertainment.com.au/

www.icmi.com.au/carol-cooke

www.greatexpectation.com.au/presenter/Resilience-speakers/Carol-Cooke-AM

COURAGE
CHANCE
CHANGE